BLOODED THOUGHT
●
Occasions of Theatre

BLOODED THOUGHT

•

Occasions of Theatre

by

HERBERT BLAU

•

Performing Arts Journal Publications
New York City

Library of Congress Cataloging in Publication Data
Blooded Thought
Library of Congress Catalog Card No.: 82-81976
ISBN: 0-933826-38-9
ISBN: 0-933826-39-7 (paper)

Design: Gautam Dasgupta

Printed in the United States of America

For Kathy

What do you think you'll do with all that horrible stretch of time?
Have you ever thought about it, Woyzeck?
Buchner, *Woyzeck*, Sc. 1

It must be visible or invisible,
Invisible or visible or both:
A seeing and unseeing in the eye.

The weather and the giant of the weather,
Say the weather, the mere weather, the mere air:
An abstraction blooded, as a man by thought.
Stevens, *Notes Toward a Supreme Fiction*

My thoughts be bloody, or be nothing worth!
Shakespeare, *Hamlet*, IV.iv.66

. . . whatever way you turn you have not even *started* thinking.
Artaud, *Collected Works I*

Publication of this book has been made possible in part by a grant from the
National Endowment for the Arts, Washington, D.C., a federal agency, and
public funds received from the New York State Council on the Arts.

Contents

●

Foreword

●

WHAT I AM DOING HERE IS LARGELY THEORY, THOUGH IT IS ACTIVATED by occasions. I will refer to particular theatre events, but the occasions I have in mind occur at a more elemental and indeterminable level, like subatomic particles of the event. I will not have much to say of the old social occasions of theatre when people gathered (so we are told) as a community to remember, through the enactment of a dramatic narrative, the maybe half-forgotten signals of a common set of values and the venerable features of a collective fate. It hardly needs saying that there is no contemporary theatre of any consequence which is conceived for the gathering of an audience with such expectations. It is far more likely to be true that when we have contemporary theatre of the greatest consequence, it is going to have some trouble gathering an audience. That is certainly true in this country. When the audience does gather in the accustomed spaces, it seems more like a collective desire to forget or, with a lapse of memory about where we are in history, for the perpetuation of the most exhausted illusions. To the extent that it still reflects human nature, the theatre is practiced in deceiving itself, for better or worse, and I will want to speak about those illusions without which—in an age of demystifications—there can be no theatre of any consequence.

At the center of any critical theory today, not only in the theatre, is the problematic of the audience. "Who's there?" The issue is raised in the opening words of *Hamlet*, the play whose symptoms are almost a definition of modernity, with its swarm of percussive questions in the play-within-the-play. Not only who? but where? and why? and in what space of thought? in the superstructure or the cellarage? When we think of an audience today, we are not only concerned with the numbers in attendance, but the attentiveness to an absence, the presence of otherness in the process of watching, the watching and being watched, estrangement and distance—and the degree to which *division*, the unstable substance of theatre, mirrored in the event, has since become its subject. The problem at that limit is a solipsistic anxiety that *nobody may be looking*, which has become, through an inversion of the voyeuristic fear we see in Kafka, a paranoid constituent of the performing self.

Not only have we wanted to breach the distance of estrangement by playing back the subject in self-reflexive structures, reducing the quotient of otherness in the event, but it also seems that the more the audience is reduced, or seems to disappear, the more strenuously we urge it to participate. The invitation is subtler in recent performance than it was in the sixties, with its communitarian dream of everybody performing, but the audience is inevitably of two minds, drawn in and stopping short. If the exhortations to participate have abated, the *dream* has not entirely disappeared. The truth seems to be that it can't disappear, since it is consanguineous with the theatre, part of its substance, though in recent years—as the public spectacle receded and returned to speculation—it has been displaced into theory, which plays itself out in the metamorphoses of language. I am thinking, as I do in the essays which make up the book, of how the performance principle has come to possess, along with the play of language, not only the other arts, but philosophy, linguistics, psychoanalysis, anthropology and—as if it were the space of a Total Theater composed of all these—the most advanced literary theory.

One of the major concerns of the book is language in the theatre, and its absence, or the appearance of it—for even when the theatre was programmatically non-verbal, it was acting out of a kind of deflected and unknowing obeisance to the unremembered word. If I might indulge a verbal shift to follow up the subject, the occasions I have in mind might also be thought of as *occlusions*. What I am thinking of, specifically, in complicating the occasion with this play upon it, is that momentary closure in the vocal tract when, as on the ramparts, the breath catches, and stops, and then releases out—under pressure, perhaps, of the need to say it. It is no accident that there was an almost manic obsession over the last generation with the voice and *voicing*, with actors driven back to the source for the right to say it. "Nay, answer me. Stand and unfold yourself." Mostly, it seemed, the self could only stammer.

But since we're out on the ramparts, where the air bites shrewdly and the atmosphere is charged with ontological confusions: I am also thinking of that occluded front in meteorology when the cold front overtakes the warm and forces it above the earth's surface, as my own accumulated experience of theatre has been overtaken and—through the work's stoppage and a disposition to theory—forced full body into abstraction. I hope it will be, as Wallace Stevens says of a poem, a "blooded abstraction." An occlusion is also a stoppage of the blood. When the blood occludes in a vein, you may die; when the bleeding occludes in a wound, you may live. Concerned as it has been with living and dying, there is something occluded in the theatre that is not conclusive. As Hamlet says of good and bad, thinking makes it so. According to Freud, the thinking is in-terminable, because it is the unceasing displacement of the memory of gratification. It is at that generic level—suggested by their common etymological roots—that theatre reflects theory. From the beginning, apparently, it was a blooded abstraction. And to the extent that my theorizing reflects its subject, this is far from being a book of conclusions.

Whatever its origins—and whatever we mean by an audience—that quality of experience we call *theatre* is a kind of occulted occasion. I suppose I hear something like the condensation of that idea in the Joycean play of the word occlusion, with a further echo of *collusion*, as in the occasion we call *drama*. The drama is naturally enough, in our tradition, identified with theatre, almost synonymously, but it is important to remember they are not the same. We are now far more aware than we used to be of other traditions of theatre in which the drama is minimal or (nearly) absent. We have also had experimental forms of theatre in recent years, or Performance Art, and considerable theory, working off the conviction that the theatre is occluded by drama, and that we might very well have a better theatre without it, and with that, a better world, since the drama is the long illuded story of *mis*-representation; in political terms, the authorized record of our self-deceptions, impacted by mimesis, recycled, and performed in life.

I shall have occasion in these essays to say more about that reproductive process, and about the practice of *deconstruction*, in which the delusions of drama are theoretically broken down into an infinitely widening field of gratuitous play, thereby relieving the world of the false appearances of theatre by dispersing them, somewhat paradoxically, into the nature of theory. It is very impressive theory for all that. In the theatre itself, we see in deconstructed versions of the dramatic text the working out of a dilemma which has, again paradoxically, been dramatized by the history of modernism: that is, whether the drama is fake or not; and not only that, but whether there is too much theatre in life; indeed, whether there is too much theatre in the theatre; and what determines more or less. This problem has been complicated since the sixties by our growing awareness of the theatricalizing of everyday life, so that all occasions seem to inform against the theatre, diffusing the power of the specific theatrical occasion into an epistemological field of mere *seeming*.

It is in the interstices of that impermeable problem, through which all perception nevertheless leaks, that the occasion interests me, "If it be,/ Why seems it so particular with thee?" "Seems, madam? Nay, it is. I know not 'seems.' " The theatre exists, it seems to me, in a kind of no man's land between duplicity and opacity. I have wanted—in the theatrework I've done and in this book—to think through (*by means of?*) the difference with almost Hamletic particularity. I will be looking through the seeming not merely to the specific occasion, but to the specificity of the *occasioning*, the incitement *to* theatre which comes, as it shares its reality with life, of *too much theatre*, the critical momentariness of the gathering of theatre in thought as audience of its own process until, it seems, there is *nothing but* theatre, but (again) in stubborn contradistinction to the world, which only appears to be theatre. "Fie upon't, foh! About, my brains." It is a state of mind occluded with the thought of theatre. It is what, in the desire to strike through the appearance of opacity, makes one almost hate the theatre in the thought about it. Yet what moves me in the theatre is precisely that, the power of theatre *as thought*, which thought without theatre cannot approach. It is that which seems to move theorists in other disciplines towards the theatre, say a Barthes or a Derrida. I think Aristotle was on to it when he wrote of theatre combining the powers of philosophy and history, though Plato warned about the seeming that would overtake them both. It is, nevertheless, this power of theatre I was thinking of when, in one of the essays, I named it "The Thought of Performance."

So far as it can go, the *idea* of theatre is—in its most carnal embodiments—to de-realize or de-materialize the world, though the most powerful thought of theatre, what drives the theatre mad, is that the world only lets it go so far. Or, as Shakespeare kept saying and unsaying, in the plays, in the sonnets, in the worst puns upon his given name, the world's inviolable divisions are derisive of the theatre's will. Which is why there is a kind of brain fever in the occasion, inseparable from the theatre's future, which is the divided subject of the last essay, "Flights of Angels, Scattered Seeds." There is also, in the transitory nature of the form, the thought that what is being occluded is so subtle, or subtilized, that it has little more substance than the momentary breath, breath-*taking*—which reminds us again that the theatre is an occasion which exists most substantially in the rehearsal of its disappearance. I rehearse that notion, and the dynamics of vanishing, in more than one essay; and in one of them—reflecting on how time out of mind the theatre is clued into presence by the elusiveness of language—I settle on a word between occlusions and occasions when I speak of *precipitations* of theatre. What I am thinking of there is at least a double meaning of the word: the precipitation which occurs in the movement of occluded fronts, a condensation of *imminence*; and the precipitousness with which it might occur, "as swift/As meditation or the thought of love," the subjunctive fine suddenness of the occasion, acute as a "stricken deer" or abrupt as a "crooked eclipse." (The mathematicians have been trying to describe such moments in what they now call Catastrophe Theory.) It is then—as with the occlusion of time in the language of the unconscious, the *imprint* of an absence—that we become aware of what we finally *see* in the theatre, those"waste blanks" which consummately absorbed Shakespeare, and Beckett, and of which I speak, relating the performance principle to the Reality Principle in the afterimages of recent experiment, in "Look What Thy Memory Cannot Contain."

Film, of course, has tried to contain it, but without the occlusions of theatre, in the empty but continuous signifiers of the cinematic space, as if the waste blanks were left in the editing room. But that is only the filmic illusion, with its high degree of apparent reality and low degree of actual existence. I examine that illusion, and what film theorists call "the scopic drive," in an essay on "Theatre and Cinema," focusing the issue in a specular distinction between the curtain and the screen, what you see there and what you don't, in the circling longevity of projected desire, like the uninterrupted recurrency of an eclipse. Not all theatres have a curtain, but all theatre remembers that it was there. It also remembers—in various repressed and involuted ways—when it *wasn't* there, the possiblity of *closure*, of which the curtain is emblematic and, even when not there, still momentary in the mind. There is more on the cinematic apparatus in the final essay (or series of mini-essays, a sort of organum of the postmodern), as there is on the dematerialization of technology and its relationship to theatre, with its unstanched desire for something like the seeming undividedness of film, the fantasy of an uninterrupted present, like the timelessness of the unconscious, which remembers what we forget.

Throughout the book, I will be exploring a certain *momentariness* in theatre, defined by Shakespeare in his sonnets, where the thought of theatre is drawn like film so finely through its own processes of speculation that it seems to be occurring in the unconscious. It's almost as if in the vertigo of reflection the abstraction were drained of blood, seeming then to pass beyond perception, though it's all taking place, bodily, in front of your eyes. It's hard to say about such moments whether we are dealing with occasions or occlusions, a closure or a crossing. If we run the film back in the mind's eye to get our bearings, we find ourselves retracing the long oedipal history of theatre to the place where, in a dazzle of abstraction, three roads meet, and the superfluity of play ac-

quires another dimension—as at the "dream's navel" (Freud). Is it also
the place where, in the speculative dazzle of another moment of
theatre, prayers cross? Since I look at our recent devotion to ritual occasions with a skeptical eye, I am somewhat reluctant to speak in the
old mythic and hierophantic terms about the theatre being reborn at
such disjunctures. I prefer to speak of a remembered occasion. It seems
to me always the same dream dreaming within itself the encircled
wound of *representation*. That leads, as in analysis, to interpretation
which never ends. It is the superfluity that I am concerned with—like
the unoccluded blood in a wound or the unstopped sound in the throat
or random particles of air—in the essay on "The Remission of Play,"
which also gives a view of what's been happening in the theatre, and
out of the theatre, in the period since the sixties. In the still-current
fetishism of play—and the supersaturation of performance as a mode
of thought or a way of life—the essay wonders about remission as you
would for a disease. Since in thought, at least, I suffer from it, as the
essay will make more apparent, what I say about the disease is hardly
conclusive. A distrust of the widespreading attenuation of performance
nurtures other ambivalences in the book.

In my resistance to the new orthodoxies of play, there is a pattern of
very equivocal feelings, and my own illusions; and a sense of play with
another mission. If I sometimes feel that the powers of play are grossly
overrated in the serious business of the world, I am not denying—since
I've known it in the theatre—that dizzying excess of play whose limit is
indeterminable, when the breath does catch in the throat and releases
itself to an occasion where, if something is not born again, it is being
indelibly remembered. I also think that's serious business. I tend to
believe, whatever the play, that the theatre is better in the remembrance than in the birthing, though I have been sufficiently saturated
with what it remembers—the trace of the ritual occasions of an
originary drama—that I may in one or another sentence of the essays
relinquish my skepticism to the premonition of a regressive thought,
that *for*getting of theatre which is, as in the dream-wish of Artaud, a
sonorous intimation of pure play. I am very much concerned in several
of these essays with innovation in the theatre, and I have spent much of
my life at it, but I would not be the first to admit that—so far as I can
see in our theatre today—such breathtaking moments are exceedingly
rare. If our theatre seems wanting at less precipitous moments, I think
it has something to do with our conception of play.

Aside from being concerned with what incites the theatre at its most
subliminal levels, these essays were also written for occasions, which
you may find in the acknowledgments. Despite the fact that some of

them were written to be spoken, there are moments when the style may seem occluded. In a period of theatre which has been sometimes quite indifferent to language, even abusive, I have tried in my own theatrework to be very attentive to words, as I've tried to be in this book. If there's something elliptical in the attention, I might cite as a justifying model the self-recursive playfulness of recent critical theory, although that model has been derived, as I've already indicated, from theory's activated remembrance of its aboriginal affinity with theatre. More about the personal implications in a moment. About the place of theory in our theatre, let me not be misleading. We have in this country no tradition of theoretical discourse, as there is in France or Germany—or for that matter, as it has developed recently in our other visual arts, which have gone through a Conceptual period into Performance.

Some of that rubbed off on our theatre, but insufficiently so to keep me from feeling at times that these are rather dispossessed reflections. It would be nice if the essays elicited some diacritical response from closet theorists and practitioners both. One wants the corrective friction of congenial thought. Or even an occasional battle of ideas. What I'm saying and how I'm saying it would be reasonably familiar abroad within the stylistic dispensation of the "human sciences," which appropriated theatricality as a method and gave it back to the theatre as a matrix, through the ideological exchanges after the sixties. The "Theatrum Philosophicum" of which Michel Foucault speaks in *Language, Counter-Memory, Practice* is just about second nature to various French directors who were weaned during that period. Our practice, however, is still distrustful of theory. So much the better for the practice? Maybe so. But one might think twice about that when looking around for, say, something comparable to the remarkable subversion of Wagner's *Ring* at Bayreuth, the "continuous *hermeneutic* shock," as one critic put it, conceived of by Boulez and Chéreau within the sociopolitical matrix of the theoretical discourse.

As for the *scale* of productive experiment in Germany today, which I shall discuss briefly within, it is made possible not only by the resources of the state theatre system but by a generation of theatre artists whose theoretical awareness ranges from Adorno and Saussure to Habermas and Lacan and is lightyears apart from the relative indifference to ideas, not to mention political thought, in our Regional Theatres. A short time ago, when I was in Germany, I was invited for an informal conversation with the directors, and some of the actors, of the Staatstheater in Stuttgart, whose work is audacious and controversial. There were *five* Dramaturgs present (another couldn't make it), which is like having a rather formidable think-tank within the theatre, with power to determine its policy and critical jurisdiction over the radically edited texts. (Specimens of the texts are analyzed in the splendidly documented programs which are prepared for each production like scholarly monographs.) Almost everybody present had travelled fairly widely in the United States, observing theatre, respectful of some of the acting and some of the scattered experiment. The question they asked me, however, to kick off the discussion was why are we so "ideologically unconcerned" with what our actors are asked to speak, and did I think it would be worse in a period of conservative retrenchment? I didn't think it would be worse but I couldn't say it would be better under an actor-president whose dominant theory is supply-side economics, which apparently depends, as our theatres already do, on predicting the psychology of the public.

The German theatres are by no means exempt from that, nor from the political pressures that go with a more predictable subsidy. But they benefit from a discourse that is not available to us, and it was enlivening to talk about theatre with people who are thinking about it and doing it at that theoretical level. As for recent critical theory, if I have no aversion to its style, I am not aiming either, in entering the discourse, to disperse meanings through a "galaxy of signifiers" within a "field of infinite difference" in order to produce like Roland Barthes a "writerly text" reflecting myself writing through "the infinite play of the world" which, as Barthes cautions, is always in danger of being intersected by ideology or occluded by a system. As I've also indicated, I have some misgivings about the ideology of play. My instincts are rather to say what I mean as exactingly as I can, taking my chances with closure, although I can't help recognizing that—if the model of thought is the theatre—the meanings will inevitably disperse themselves in the genotext of the form, the invisible writing of the actor's body, that recessive and dilatory instrument of a dubious presence. I shall say more about that, which is a complicated subject (the name, the content), related to the indeterminacies of dream-thought.

If meanwhile I think of the writing as a performance—saying and unsaying, always approximating, recessive, digressive, a metonymic labor—it's because I want to be as responsible to the thought of performance as performance must be when most credible to itself. I have wished sometimes I could say the same thing in different words. But I grew up in a climate of thought about language, pre-structuralist, in which I was convinced, as I still am, that you can't say the same thing in different words. Different words, different thing. And the same thing is true of doing without words, or merely playing around with them, as in the polydipsic poesis of much postmodern performance;

and a single gesture is not, despite the popular wisdom and some acting theory, worth a thousand words, for that still depends upon the words, and your sense of language as a gesture. Whatever the gesture is worth, it is quite a different thing. The theatre has suffered during the last generation from the illusion that such a thing might be naturally superior. The best of modern poetry has taught us that the words are about things that wouldn't exist without the words. I believe the same might be said of the language of theatre, a concept which wouldn't exist without the memory of words.

I have tried to keep that in mind in writing these essays, but among the things that memory cannot contain is what post-structuralist thought is obsessed with: the scattered image of words sounding, in the air and the inner ear: the inaccessible dimensions of the signifiers, and the bodily gestures in which the words are always already inscribed: the structure of the signifiers which operates according to the causality of the unconscious, itself a language; and the ceaseless desire of being which always escapes the movement of the sign which *is* the divided and dividing subject of theatre. That doesn't mean you don't struggle to keep it from escaping, even by the decoy of a determining passivity that lets it take its course. So with the words on the page, where the forgetting or short-circuitry of meaning is neither an alibi nor a dodge, but a stringency of thought. As in the theatre, all you can do is assure the other—actor, audience, perhaps the mirrored and mirroring self—that what is *being-said* and what is *being-thought* are, with all the intelligence of the thinking body, given over to the occasion. False ambiguity, evasion, or obscurantism are never intended, though to avoid the intentional fallacy you've tried to discipline a craft. The occasion may be, however, of a particular order of complexity which may be right at the conceptual edge of your powers of thought, maybe slipping over with the signifying chain.

I am often dealing here with issues of theatre which, though I've been pursuing them for over thirty years, are always at the moment of apprehension passing out of sight. Like subatomic particles, that seems to be their nature. I want very much to stay with them. The words evince the reaching, but their nature seems to be the same.

Since what I am saying of words is very close to my conception of theatre, let me say it again, if not simply, in rather simple words: in what I have to say the way I say it is the *thought* of what I'm saying. If there were any other way to say it, I would, but I would be saying something else. I may be saying something else no matter what I say, which is what I'm saying. If the thought is circular now as well as occluded, I believe it came to be that way from many years of thinking *in* the theatre, attempting to get as close to the thought of theatre as theatre would be if in a conspiracy of illusion and history (we have left the simple words) it were thinking about itself. It seems to me that during the course of its history the theatre has been doing just that, worrying about the illusion and wondering if it's history, therefore never quite sure what it's worrying about. I will be worrying about that in these essays. The illusion from which I suffer, perhaps, is that my thought is by now inseparable from the thought of performance. Which remains to be seen.

Even if it should turn out not to be an illusion, *that* illusion, then one might worry—as Marx did in his famous last thesis on Feuerbach—about another, which identifies consciousness with performance. "The philosophers have only *interpreted* the world," he wrote, "in various ways; the point, however, is to *change* it." Brecht agreed, taking the point for granted. But they have started to argue again about what exactly Marx meant, and long before Marx, and despite Brecht, about the degree to which consciousness does change the world. The appearance of the world's stubborn presence leads to the conjecture that the world's stubborn presence is *nothing but appearance*. The raising of consciousness to that impasse is not altogether comforting. As Hamlet guessed, there may be nothing harder to change than the dominion of appearance. Yet he also knew in his heart the difference between thinking and doing, once he had done it.

Years ago, in a gesture of hubris, I wrote that I was working in the theatre in order to save the world. I am not at the moment working in the theatre, but I still can't think of any better motive for being there. Need I add that, while I *think* of the theatre, as I speak of it here, as an activity of consciousness—an almost pure conceptual event in a world of stubborn appearance—I have no illusions in the day-by-day *making* of theatre, where I have had occasion for bloody thoughts, that it can be blooded with nothing but thought.

Acknowledgements

●

There are a few interpolations after the fact, and some other minor revisions, but the essays are just about as they were for the particular occasions. If I start out reflecting on the divided worlds of theatre, that's because the audience for the first essay, "The Thought of Performance," was sure to be divided, with some very distant from the newer forms of theatre. That essay was prepared for a symposium at Loyola University of Chicago in November 1979. The proceedings were subsequently published in *Modern Theater: A Reflection of Twentienth Century Man and Society?*, edited by John T. Trahey and Jonathan C. Wilson. "The Remission of Play" was written for a more homogeneous audience of theorists and critics, more or less aware of what was new, at the First International Conference on Innovation/Renovation, held in Germany in June 1980. The conference was sponsored by the University of Würzburg in cooperation with the University of Munich and the United States International Communications Agency. The essay will also appear in a volume edited by Ihab and Sally Hassan, to be published in Germany, and in this country by the University of Wisconsin Press. "Precipitations of Theatre" appeared in the Autumn 1980 issue of *New Literary History* and "Look What Thy Memory Cannot Contain" in the April 1981 issue of *Bennington Review*. The essay on "Theatre and Cinema" was delivered at the annual film conference of the Center for 20th Century Studies at the University of Wisconsin—Milwaukee in March 1980. Those conferences are highly theoretical, with a heavy bias of what is called French Freud. The papers from that conference were published in the Winter 1981 issue of *Ciné-Tracts*, edited by Patricia Mellencamp.

The last essay and the last completed, "Flights of Angels, Scattered Seeds," was commissioned for a projected issue of *The Drama Review* on The Theater of the Future. The issue was unfortunately cancelled but not, I trust, the future. My wife Kathleen Woodward wouldn't particularly stand for that, no more than she does for the minutest editorial lapse in a manuscript. I am thankful, too, for her fastidious listening. My research assistant, Eleanor Honig Skoller, became something of a confidant as she agreeably carried out the nuisance tasks around the earliest indeterminacies of the ideas that eventually went into the essays. The earliest indeterminacies of my work in the theatre, and my writing about it, were encouraged long ago by Robert W. Corrigan, when he was founding editor of the original *Drama Review*. He has seen them generously through every phase of my career in the theatre, as well as various manuscripts and public controversy. While some of the thinking here has been evolving as long as I've been in the theatre, the more demanding nuances of theory are indebted, like everything I've written recently, to the work I was fortunate to do with the members of the KRAKEN group.

I am also very grateful to Bonnie Marranca and Gautam Dasgupta, editors of *Performing Arts Journal*, for their responsiveness to my theoretical work and for suggesting that they would publish it if I made the essays into a book.

H.B.
May 1981

BLOODED THOUGHT

●

Occasions of Theatre

The Thought of Performance:

Value, Vanishing, Dream, and Brain Damage

●

IN THE CORROSIVE AND EQUIVOCAL NIHILISM OF *THE WILL TO POWER*, Nietzsche generalizes what, if one looks to cases, seems plainly inarguable: "Feelings about values are always behind the times; they express conditions of preservation and growth that belong to times long gone by; they resist new conditions of existence with which they cannot cope and which they necessarily misunderstand; thus they inhibit and arouse suspicion against what is new." In our time, with a now-established Tradition of the New, we must cope with another suspicion: that we don't know how to resist. Our feelings about values are mostly unattached feelings or feelings of no-value, making for abdication of judgment. It takes a radical sort of reticence not to be intimidated by quick seizures of fashion, all the more because fashion is so cunningly gifted. I say this with reticence, because as soon as you give an inch in this direction, you're liable to encourage the misunderstanders. There are those—persuaded neither by fashion nor the long blush of error in rejections of modern art—who are only too willing to have further grounds for the wrong resistance. There are some who are unregenerate, and it makes no difference what you encourage or what you don't. Along with the plain junk, they can also be ignored.

I am troubled, rather, by something else—the imposing plenitude of change that, if you think twice, seems to return us to the same old stalemates. There are times when it all seems unregenerate, change but a deceit of fantasy in the status quo, serving its unbudgeable purpose. If you really think again, the trouble is the profusion, containing as it does varieties of the meritricious that are undeniably beguiling. It takes a cold eye for the fact in order to take its measure. What you're looking for is the work which, if it isn't reflecting new conditions of existence (because suspicious of the reflections?), is nevertheless determined to shake up the unchangeable. Such an alternative may be the margin between accepting things as they are because they *appear* to change, and the indefinite replication of the illusion that they *do*, because even if they do it often appears they don't.

Which is not quite what Nietzsche meant by the return of the Same. The Eternal Recurrence which plays through *The Birth of Tragedy* is a persistent fantasy of the theatre. It dreams of renewal by the recurrency of a Source, even as (at the base of all values) the ground starts slipping and origins disappear. It is the ontological crisis behind the Energy Crisis. It's hard to think about the theatre and not think about that, particularly as we turn to myth and ritual in order to avoid thinking about history. Or talk about theatre as theatre in order to avoid thinking at all.

I start with these reflections because when we talk about theatre we are often talking about quite different worlds of theatre (to pluralize a title by Robert Corrigan). It may very well be a single universe, but there are lightyears between the galaxies. As for the galaxies beyond theatre, towards which we look from a polluted star, is there a certain vanity of thought in the prospect that intelligent beings elsewhere are waiting to hear from us, or trying to communicate? Why should they want to? I don't say this cynically, but we are embarrassed by history. Before we speak of renewal in the theatre, perhaps we should remember the conditions of existence which put all renewal in doubt. It's the least we can do for history, of which the theatre is a symptom as well as the mirror. Long before OPEC, and in whatever period, the Energy Crisis was the *generic* subject matter of theatre, in tragedy or comedy, whether the plague in Thebes, the rottenness in Denmark, the lost valise in Victoria Station, the crack in the chimney of the Master Builder or—on the offchance that the nightmare of history may be only a bad dream (only?), the worst returning to laughter—the Imaginary Invalid, Molière's or Beckett's. Even if it's not there, it's *there* (what? what "beats there," says the hallucinating Lear on the heath), whether blocked, repressed, paranoiacally excluded, or on the selvedge of consciousness like a troubled ghost, in the psychopathology of everyday life.

As the theatre holds its mirror up to nature, somewhat fractured for what it sees—the mere reflective *image* having such force ("Cover her face, mine eyes dazzle . . .")—we return to the thought with which I started, the feelings about values that resist the new conditions, the more distressing thought (unacceptable to Brecht) that they may not really be *new*, but irreparably there, or inevitably, from the beginning; a suspicion to worry about and argue about in the discourse of history. There is also that other discourse that may not be possible, because of the distance between those working in the theatre, where words fly up and thoughts remain below—the worlds separated by uncrossable multiples of the speed of light.

Putting the best complexion on the distance: we may be equally intelligent beings but with unalterably different concerns in an unstable cosmos of mutually cancelling values. We can't say. Silence is not golden, however, it is the pit and the pendulum, the murmur of history below the flow of words. Out of some compulsion one speaks into the Void, which may be after all the authorizing medium of speech, the most anointed and uncontaminated space of communion. Nietzsche thought so, and some of the more attentive theologians trying to revive the God he proclaimed dead, a victim of brain damage, about Whom (and the concept of Man that appears to be dying with Him) we are liable to feel as we do about cardiac arrest in the intensive care ward, no more to be done, have mercy, pull the plug. As Heidigger said, following Nietzsche, the dreadful thing has already happened—and will, I'm afraid, continue to.

Whatever the thing is, it lurks in the background of thought (as in the theatrework I have done) as a sort of indeterminate datum of a testing of values. As for the brain damage involved, we will return to that specifically in another context, where metaphysics passes into therapy by grace of performance. In performance, values are physiological, cutting to the brain, affects of power, freedom, ease, displeasure, exuberance, incapacity, pride, grief, the expression of sustaining or inhibited life, aspects of release or self-mortification, maybe even joy-in-grief, which others proclaim though few of us experience it, more likely to feel exhaustion, pity, outrage, self-pity or a sense of relief, which runs like a spasm through our systems of value—like Nietzsche's thought. "Our most sacred convictions," he writes, "the unchanging elements in our supreme values, are judgments of our muscles."

There's a sense in which talking about performance outside of performance, especially some new types of performance, is like talking about UFOs. Maybe you see it maybe you don't. If something was there, we're not sure what—nor exactly how, in what form, whether as substance or apprehension, the thing itself or speculation, specular, *put there by thought*, dis-appearance or mere delusion. I mean that the idea of disappearance is engrailed in the very nature of theatre. Now you see it now you don't. The disappearing is apparent. (Parse the word and there is a *parent*, familiar, the source toward which appearance moves, *apparency*, the presence of an origin which is not-there.) In the twentieth century it has become, through apparencies of inturned thought—the reflexive play within the play—the self-conscious subject of the form. The theatre has done a lot of thinking about performance in the act of performance. It has been done in both superficial and excruciating ways, in *The Balcony* or *The Screens*, or in *Rosencrantz and Guildenstern*. In the experimental theatre, it is usually without what makes it excruciating, but at different levels of emotional or perceptual complexity, as in the distances between The Open Theater, the Ontological Hysteric Theater, and Mabou Mines.

I suppose it was Pirandello who, making an explicit issue of what was always equivocally there, forced us to attend to the manifest content of the latency in performance: the idea of performance thinking about itself; so much so that we can hardly imagine a time anymore when it was not doing so. The six characters searching for an Author were, moreover, also searching for an identity *as* characters, in a virtually untellable story that could only repeat itself as if the characters were mere subjects of the *repetition*, which was always transgressing the distinctiveness of their roles. As for the actors watching—neither person nor role—what else could they be but astonished (if they really gave it thought) because who, then, were they as they watched? mere objects? then subjects? and the others watching them watching, who were they? the persons in the auditorium, objects or subjects of the confusion? Not all the plays you see are as specifically tautological as that (some are without knowing it), but that's what you're likely to think about plays, and not only plays, if you think at all, that's the trouble with thinking—which Pirandello's actors, who were no more than rather sketchy characters, wanted to keep out of the theatre, as some of our actors do, with more or less success.

Be that as it may, as soon as thought gets into performance, the central problem of drama becomes what is already intrinsic to theatre (they are not the same, drama and theatre, though we equate the words): knowing what there *is* to be performed. Do it again, we say in rehearsal, in unconscious testament to an Eternal Recurrence. The Same, but not quite. Do *what*, however? The characters don't know, and maybe shouldn't. How can the actors be sure? The director is guessing. The play's the thing, we used to say, as if we knew what the play was.

Well, there was fairly good reason for that. There used to be a time, as with the Sacred, when we could go back to the Book and check our interpretation. The Text was the inseminating source to which we were to show fidelity, line perfect, deferring to the Author as if he were God the Father. Pirandello tipped us off that something was wrong when those dispossessed characters appeared on the stage with their runaway obsessions looking for the interpretation they couldn't find because the director really couldn't be trusted and the Author was seemingly missing. But only seemingly. Pirandello couln't resist writing himself in, but even if he wrote himself out the seeming would remain. Absence is relative. One of the disturbing tendencies of our last generation of theatre practice was to take the idea even further, undermining the Authority of the Text, which was revised, scissored, reviled and—along with the Author—even tossed out of the theatre now and then. In the sixties what we tried to liberate was the actor's body, non-verbal, anti-verbal, or partially and spastically verbal, in the regressively assertive texts of collectively created events, where sound and movement dominated, with words as texture perhaps. When words were used, they were often parody since they couldn't be trusted either (or as we later came to feel, the actors couldn't trust themselves). The language had been invalidated by the lie of history, with its myth about the beginning as a Word.

During this period we weren't performing dramas, but *theatre pieces*: montage, *bricolage*, action events. If not drama, still play, *structures* of play, more or less improvisational, or ideographic increments of a theme. They were certainly not *productions* in the old sense (and the idea of *producing texts* by theoretical labor had still to be clarified in another scene). That word was associated with the bourgeois production process, the institutional framework of theatre, higher finance, expensive mountings, and the contemptible use-value of the commodity system that was buying up the Spirit of Play. Brecht had called it "culinary theatre" where if you can afford it you put it on your expense account, digest your dinner and go to sleep, secure in the knowledge that you aren't missing anything, for the Text (whatever the surface differences) repeats itself below the eyelids with the serial monotony of ideological sameness, like Andy Warhol's silkscreened soups. The new structures of play were primarily for those who couldn't afford the other; they were meant to be marginal, dissident, unprivileged and cheap. But they soon had their brand names, too, a standard ideology, rising prices, and adaptable gestures. The games, transformations, communitarianism, and transactional behavior of that period could be, and were, easily appropriated, like *Hair*, by the omniverousness of the consumer apparatus. The exercises of the New Theatre went rapidly into the fashions of the Counter-Culture and onto the bourgeois market, or into old-valued productions that were pretending to be something else, like *A Chorus Line*, which apparently started with something like the revelations of a T-group around an absent text.

The Text had been disputed or abandoned because it was held to be the proprietary seat of established value. Authority was in the way. Actor and Act had to be liberated from prescription. The desire for unmediated experience is still as it was in The Living Theater, one of the complex and honorable motives of our romantic tradition. I do not mean to slight the intelligence and dedication of the experiments when I say they left us with a *surface* that could easily be confiscated. Part of the problem was that in rejecting the invisible depths—and hence ideological bias—of the Text, we were left with little but surface, and that much less intelligence. Whatever the case, the unmediated Spirit of Play was, it seems, quickly exhausted. And then there is the question of what, in a culture of accommodations, is *not* appropriable by the system.

In the seventies, the written text was in again. There were characters once more in reasonable facsimiles of the old plots. There were actors, as ever, in search of a job. Many were so disheartened by the disappointment of ingenuous expectancies in the New Theatre—or so ingenuously celebrated in the quick euphoria—that they went straight to Hollywood where, on commercials, soaps, and in the movies, there is the one infinitely replicated immutable Text which is the enviable summary of all desire, where character is canonical and determinable as a single role. As for the polymorphous thinking body which had for a while in the theatre displaced the Text, it was coming to discover that, along with the unreliable duration of group consciousness, it had a limited repertoire of ideas. In the Age of Aquarius, this included the appealing notion of Love's Body, running out of postures as of politics, somewhat bruised in the pleasuring of soul, having forgotten (what Yeats didn't, what Nietzsche didn't) that the values in our muscles are still attached to our minds which, even if blown, are made of language. If words could fail us, as they undeniably did, they are also, if the mind is put to it, the conceptualizing power by which we grasp, as Marx puts it (using the same German root for *grasp* and *concept*), the presence of history's structure in its effects. This is not what is meant by the Collective Unconsciousness which, if it exists at all, serves us right.

One of the effects of our recent history, needing still to be understood *in* the theatre, is the sharpened discourse over the authority of the Text. That discourse, if you think about it, crosses the lines between theatre and the other arts, and between theatre and the other disciplines which, paradoxically, appear to be emulating the theatre as a model of inquiry, with the idea of performance at the epistemological center. (It should be clear that I think of theatre in that sense as a discipline.) It really wasn't a matter of epistemology, however, that in the cooled-down conservative holding action of the seventies, the Text was back. It was not so much theory as compensation for the excesses. Now, when you experiment with the classics, you have to be careful. You risk the chastening assault of a Sunday column in the New York *Times*. Academic scholarship—which was always discomfited by Shakespeare our Contemporary—feels doubly fortified, since it also believes what it reads in the newspapers. The spirit of critical charity, if not puerile celebration, that indulged the off-off-Broadway-La Mama-Third Theatre boom, has gone through an embarrassed subsidence with the ending of the Vietnam War. Those who had sponsored in the sixties, on behalf of protest, far worse depredations on the dramatic literature, and intelligence, are rising now on behalf of the Text like guardians of the ring-hoard. That is not the discipline I was talking about.

Let me approach the problem this way: so far as performance goes, the Text remains our best evidence *after* the fact, like the quartos and folios of the Elizabethan stage. There is still, however, the question of the nature of the Text *before* the fact. Not only *how* do you do it? and *what* are you doing? *why*? but *where does it come from? and how much of it is really there?* that is, how far behind the text does the Text extend? or, through subtext and annotation, the leaping forward of retrospection? Truism: you can hardly get a performance out of a book. But then, having seen many performances done *by* the presumable book—with sworn faithfulness to the dramatic literature—I have also preferred them *in* the book. I mean: I am not the only person working in the theatre who sometimes feels (more often than not if the truth were known) that I *do* theatre because I don't much like going to plays. They are almost invariably—especially if the Text is great—so much less than a reductive shadow of the magnitude in the mind.

I realize that's a presumption (and there are rare exceptions). But it's also a ubiquitous thought of some newly-realized consequence in the venerable tradition of dramatic theory. Nor am I the first to feel about certain imaginings of theatre that what's on stage, even if well-enacted, can never conceivably approach what—in the most illimitable theatre of all—is projected by the imagination upon itself.

Since The Watchman lay with dogwise contemplative patience on Agamemnon's roof, watching and being watched, as if awakening into time, waiting "to read the meaning in that beacon light" which would announce the fall of Troy, the act of interpretation has been enshrined in theatre, in every sacrotuberous ligament and cuneiform bone, as in the rebus-like network of our wish-fulfilling dreams. "The sea is there," says Clytemnestra, "and who shall drain its yield?" We follow the trail of meaning from the wine-dark sea down the purple carpet to the "red act" of the unspeakably bloody deed. (The pun may be in the translation, but it's the act that needs the reading.) The mantic elders of the Chorus say, "Grant meaning to these appearances," as the blooded abstractions of history recede into myth, "the oar blade's fading footprint . . ."—or is it a stain of myth upon history? As we endure the long aetiological journey to the founding of the Areopagus, where the hard bisexual intelligence of Athena propounds a (dubious) judgment (which is still open to reading), do we not have to concede what was said in the beginning: "this thing is clear and you may trace it"? Which is to say: if there is any meaning it is only in the appearances which, because they recede, will always be endless, like the interpretations, as in a dream.

It's almost as if—through that first "interchange of flame and flame," in the lambency of the (translated) words—we see the Text emerge *in* history as, now, "a binding net" and, now, a "bright and dreamwise ecstasy." What *is* history?, we wonder, except these shifting indeterminacies of language playing through the interpretations and laminated further by other disappearing voices in the dream of time. "No, no, see there! What is that thing that shows?" The thing itself? Another thing? the mere imagining of the thing? The cry of Cassandra is the curse of interpretation. And sometimes, too, like the indecipherable presence of the first cry, cancelling history, "the shambles for men's butchery, the dripping floor. . . ." At which time the Text appears, as it did for Yeats, an uncontrollable mystery.

The long resonance of indeterminate time has been acting insidiously within the tradition of dramatic literature to the extent we've taken seriously the reflexive implications of the play-within-the-play, which is inevitably the play of language, words words words, that inturned syllabification of a metonymic space, where the drama interprets itself. It is—from *Hamlet* to *The Balcony*, from *Life Is a Dream* to *Apocalypsis cum Figuris*, in paratheatre or metatheatre or the latest permutation of a Happening—the theatre's profoundest mixed metaphor, subverting theatre by means of theatre, transposing the drama into dream, when it's not pretending to be life. "Is this not something more than fantasy?" Certainly it is, but we're not sure what, whether life or a dream. As Hamlet—that compulsive interpreter, the master of hermeneutics—claims before the assembled court, the thing that shows is what "passeth show," performing dreamwise in the mind. The red act, in time, became a solipsistic act, playing over and over. And we find ourselves distressed by a bewildering profusion of readings. They seem to tear the Text apart. Or, as if history had never spoken, we have a wax-in-the-ear insistence that the Text be respected as it was. But what was it? One of the problems with our theatre is that its drama was persuasive, for it kept telling us from the beginning that you couldn't really say. The less we could the more we did until, as in the Jacobean period, the drama seems saturated with language; or, as recently in our theatre, the Text seemed to disappear with the drama.

But it didn't disappear without a trace. The words showed up, dispersed, in a logorrhea of theory, as other disciplines were possessed by theatre, with more or less animus against the drama. The act of reading, we know, has become a performance. For that performance, however, the drama was too restrictive, since it seems to want closure, whatever it tells us. We want a more total theatre, at least in theory. And so there is the virtuoso interpretation of Balzac's *Sarrasine* by Roland Barthes through the critical closet scenes of his book *S/Z*: or the improvisations of Jacques Derrida upon Jean Genet in the mirroring processes of his self-reflexive *Glas*. Of course Sartre had anticipated that performance in his book on Genet, which acts out through the cannibalization of Genet the canonization of Sartre—who almost deserves it, the critical act is prodigious, as the subject (an inverted saintliness) is endless.

In *S/Z*, Barthes describes an attitude toward interpreting the Text which is exquisitely theatricalist in its deferral of the disappearing substance of theatre into thought, "a perspective . . . whose vanishing point is nonetheless ceaselessly pushed back, mysteriously opened: each (single) text is the very theory (and not the mere example) of this vanishing . . ." Barthes' definition of the "writerly"—developed from his early admiration of the "pregnant moments" in Brecht (this "crucial instant," the *gestus*, "totally concrete and totally abstract")—has had its correlatives in experimental forms of theatre, and a large influence on young theatreworkers in France. It is also a cue for the scholar and critic, certainly in the reading of drama (but not only drama), where the words on the page must be, as we used to say, fleshed out—an idea Barthes elaborates in a famous passage in *The Pleasure of the Text* about the "pulsional incidents" of writing aloud, "the language lined with flesh," muzzled, granular, libidinal, tongued, throwing "the anonymous body of the actor" into the ear, like an annunciation. Performed like that, the act of reading is pregnant indeed, more visceral than some versions of theatre. The thing we're talking about—in theatre and reading, *the thought of performance*—is carnal, skin-close, intestinal, pulsed, not superimposed upon a text. We cannot deny the critical *presence*, as with an actor—though we have known actors whose presence is not critical; and some, there in the flesh, not carnal.

"Who's there? Nay, answer me. Stand, and unfold yourself." I run the lines together because it's an almost seamless act, the impermeability of which remains to be interpreted. The endless attraction of *Hamlet* is in the infinite play of thought around the presence of a missing identity. Who is challenging whom? The roles seem to be reversed. When we read the play it seems to read us. The challenge on the ramparts is the challenge *in* the Text, *to* the actor, *on behalf of the Text*, and to the apparent viewer on behalf of the total structure of appearances which constitute the performance. While this greatest of all dramas—perhaps greatest because of the hallucinatory infolding of apparency upon itself—states the proposition with all the exactitude of the palpably obscure, any text of any consequence requires something like such response from its interpreter—even if, especially if, since the practice hasn't disappeared, there appears to be no text to begin with.

The incessantly deferring open-endedness of Barthes' perception, like the structure of *Hamlet*—like sexual foreplay lovingly prolonged—has a self-enamored improvisational instinct. But the improvisational element is not merely random or associative. It is rather the articulation of determinate vanishings, like successive ghostings of the self. I bring this up because for some academics worrying about the Text that they abuse in other ways, the word *improvisation* seems to signify everything reprehensible, even immoral, in alternative forms of theatre, an automatic sloppiness, or a loss of the distinction between art and life. But, as in Barthes, one can imagine forms of theatre in which the single closure of interpretation is refused as reductive. The structure of proliferation is meant to be *exact*. The multiplicity is scored. It is as if, in a concrete space of thought, we had highly-structured theatricalizations of theory, bringing into the mind's eye *what, until seen, cannot be thought*. "T'have seen what I have seen, see what I see." Ophelia's plaintive inadequacy to the thought of what she's seen is a virtual apothegm for critics and the perceptual act of theatre. As pure intuition, it sees feelingly the epistemological link of theatre and theory—which, however, responds at the impasse, the *root* of watching, that *it cannot be seen until thought*.

What makes it so? Thinking makes it so. Which is not to deny the reality of an external world, putting all existence into consciousness, but to turn that possibility around, as the theatre does. What both Plato and Hamlet suggest (and they didn't exactly like it) is that *to start thinking is already to be theatrical*. That is why, perhaps, Satan—who (according to the interpretation) brought consciousness into the world—may be considered the first actor, and Hamlet the most polyvalent of roles. Chekov, who knew a lot about actors' feelings, said he could not imagine Hamlet being played by an actor who wasn't highly intelligent, and he wasn't hedging the bet by meaning intelligent in a non-intellectual way. But that's to understand that the intellect is also carnal, and that cerebral (etymologically) has genital roots.

I am not siphoning off the sensory from the mental. Nor am I forgetting in all this the Spirit of Play. What I am suggesting, however, is that play—which we take to be the first principle of performance—is a *secondary* affect, another fiction. The world must first be thought to be play. I am not talking of idea-plays, but of play itself being, as Huizinga said in *Homo Ludens*, the intrusion of mind into the indeterminacy of the cosmos. *So be it, to be or not to be, let be.* I make a cadence of the occluding moments. The idea of *theatre*, and with it performance, arises in the ontological permutations. Drama fails at both ends. *So be it to be or not to be let be.* What wide concussions of playful thought! The greatest drama knows the score, which we are always likely to be forgetting, that *drama* fails at both ends—dispersed in the thought of *performance.*

But now that we've come to that distressing impasse of theory, let us turn to some examples of contemporary performance, where such ideas come more specifically into play:

In the last generation, people have watched, participated in, been excluded from or outraged by the following events. Some are now virtually classics, others are legends or heuristic rumors, the mere word of which has spurred on other experiment. Some have already changed, others are bound to change the way we think about the drama, about drama and theatre which, as I've already said, are not the same, though probably inseparable. We'll start with the most recognizable of the modern classics:

1) Two tramps wait for two or more interminable hours for somebody named Godot who never comes. According to report, a verifiable rumor (I was there), prisoners at San Quentin in California—most of whom had never seen any kind of play before—found the strange behavior quite intelligible, while others not in prison (and many in the theatre) who had seen many plays before were very put off at the time (in the late fifties). Of course, those at San Quentin were liars, thieves, perjurers, the lot of them, and they could hardly be trusted.

2) A man named Acconci—below a ramp or wedge sloping from the corner of a gallery floor—masturbated. You could hear his breathing over an amplifier. The event was called *Seedbed.*

3) Samuel Beckett, who had played upon our boredom with Godot, became a Nobel Prize winner and created an event similar to that of *Seedbed*, perhaps more desolate, perhaps not, drastically however shortening the time. The lights came up, not too much, on a stage littered with debris. Nothing happened except the sound of a deep inhale,

a cry, an exhale, and then the going out of the lights. Formally perfect. No masturbation that I could hear.

4) A much younger man named Chris Burden (the name is only accidentally allegorical) disappeared. The announcement for the event said he would disappear. Only nobody knew when or from where. Another time, when he was present and people could watch, he had himself crucified on a Volkswagen. I mean actual nails driven through actual hands. (He had no intention of getting himself killed like the man in Europe who, in another performance, with one methodical slice after another, cut off his penis; or so it was said.)

5) Another familiar classic: a pianist in white tie and tails performs 4'33" (of silence)—just that, four minutes and thirty-three seconds (of silence).

6) A man was seen falling from a 7-story building. The woman responsible was a dancer. She didn't push him. She did the choreography. As far as I know, he came down safely. He was *seen* falling, or was it merely descending?

7) A 12-hour presentation of a spectacularly visual event called *The Life and Times of Joseph Stalin* began with a five-minute wordless speech-song by Queen Victoria, played by the director's 80-year-old grandmother. People were expected to come and go during the performance, to relieve themselves literally and metaphorically, and even possibly to fall asleep. This was not preferred but was acceptable. If they managed to stay awake right on through, what they saw was best seen, perhaps, like an eternal recurrence on the edge of sleep. Despite the title, the performance did not appear to be political.

8) In a small loft in Soho, on a narrow stage arranged with scrupulous frontality, a character wearing a waterproof suit with hood and gloves threw out a coiled rope but otherwise remained motionless. A woman wearing only a blanket and carrying a long stick traced the figure made by the rope on the carpet with the point of the stick. This took quite a long time. Nothing else moved. The actors gazed at the audience. The first "character" was referred to, for reasons that no plot explains, as The Abominable Snowman. The author of the text—who also directed, designed, and choreographed the play—was seated to the right of the proscenium, slightly behind it, operating sound and lights in full view of the audience, in total control of the performance, as if he were at a space console at NASA monitoring astronauts on the moon. There are similar passages in the linked performances—as if the separate plays were part of one saga with an obsessive but absent story—of the Ontological-Hysteric Theater.

9) There was an event by a group called ACT, in which the audience was led, darkling, into a light-sealed smoke-filled room where intensely trained, highly disciplined actors could just barely be seen

circling on unicycles, like animated figures from an Ernest Trova sculpture. The smoke poured from a mechanism in the middle distance, while the actors did nothing else but circle on their single wheels.

10) Another performance had a similar physical discipline but a good deal more language, intricately choral. There was a figure of Agamemnon (not quite a character, but nearly) dying over and over, the final time with a great cry—"Ah, I am struck a deadly blow, and deep within!"—turning into a shoulder stand and a back arch, the agony of the maimed King performed with enormous physical acumen, the actor bowed backwards and balanced on back-heel and fontanelle, describing (for longer than seemed endurable) the flexed memorial of his own tomb. *Rigor mortis.* The killing of Agamemnon by Clytemnestra in the bath came in the form of a massed pulsation of language, pneumatic, impeccable, legible, and swift, a wincing blade of savagely articulated words coming at the audience like axe blows.

About all of these performances it can be said they were something-more-and-other-than-what-was-done, and yet *that* presence, the thing itself, tactile, palpable, inarguably *there*, raising conjecture of a time (or time-scheme) or an otherness which was *not*. In another dimension, what was not-there was also those aspects of theatre which, when we insist too much on the priority of the dramatic literature, we are likely to forget, even in the staging. What is weakened is the *thought* of performance. In each of these events, there is the precise appearance of a *negation*, something quite other than a negligence. The choices involved are occurring at the level of a historical subtext, with what-is-not-there in mind. The absence isn't being rejected, but reconstrued. For it is certainly apparent that every one of these performances is, in some respect, a critique of the theatre as we commonly know it. That theatre is attached to the drama as we commonly know it, tautologically, through the conventions of drama, which is being reconceived off the energies of such events. As disparate as the events are, with text, without text, *the* Text is continuous in a suffusing consciousness: the warp of remembrance in the slipstream of history.

Every primer of theatre tells us that performance is the law of realization of the drama on the page. But in the recent course of things, in the theatre and the other arts, performance itself has gone through reassessment. The *idea* of performance has become the mediating, often subversive third term in the on-again off-again marriage of drama and theatre. What seems to be synchronous is not eternal but historical and cultural. Nor is the idea of performance, on the political scale, coterminous with the bourgeois theatre, with its privileged space and quantified sense of time, which determines through a whole repertoire of calculable appearances, as definite as the price of a ticket, what we take to be naturalness or credibility in acting. In short, the presence of an actor is ideological. So is his absence or silence, or the number of actors for that matter. We may remember the caution with which Aeschylus introduced the second actor or Sophocles the third, dispersing some of the Chorus into dialogue which, when we look at a play on the page, is the natural spacing of performance that we have come to expect. It is something as elemental as David Tudor's performance of John Cage's silence or Robert Wilson's stunning mortification of motion that causes us to see again what we have forgotten, like the temporal dimension of stillness or the still-breeding thought of sound; or what we have come to take for granted in the theatre, like the idea of dialogue, which was a conceptual discovery, a seismic shift of history through individuated consciousness, not an eternal given, far from natural, divisive, strange. Indeed, it is (in our own time) not the new but the conventional which is strange and even awesome when you think it over, what we *do* take for granted. The mere raising of a curtain, for instance, is a theatre event of major consequence if it is remembered that it was once not there, and you are forced to ask what possible disjuncture of evolutionary desire—what rudimentary perversion of the old unitary communion—had realized itself when it was.

If the impact of certain events, like Cage's piece or Beckett's *Breath* (or this reflection on the curtain) seems limited to the one-shot single performance of a concept (though the curtain may divide or rise, etc., as we shall see in another essay), the conceptual implications have a certain reverberative (and ideological) power of their own. With the advent of Conceptual Art, moreover, we recognized what was becoming truer (another historical accretion, if not the whole truth) that the stage of performance is an extension, through consciousness, of the continuum of art history. The mirror held up to life is also art's reflection on art. We already speak of the drama *after* Beckett. That withered tree with its begrudging leaves is a landmark in the history of the form. As for Cage, he has had a considerable impact not only on artworks and "non-matrixed" performance, but also on some of the new drama that came out of the theatre's affiliation, since the late fifties, with new dance and mixed-media events at La Mama and the Judson Church. (I happened not to like very much of it myself, I mean the plays, but they are now part of the standard fare being studied in theatre departments, which were originally hostile—and more conventional drama has been influenced since in turn.)

Many events of the New Theatre are, we know, disjunct in structure, hybrid in nature, dissociated from easily identifiable patterns or referents. They cross one art with another metamorphically and, with more or less aggressive frequency, art with life. To that extent they remain *participatory*, although the more wholesale participatory aspirations of the sixties—such as the communitarian anarchism of The Living Theater—seem to have had their day (or are still having it in another country, like The Living Theater in Italy, where political turmoil is more accommodating to the cultural activism). Some of the newer work, as it enters the systems of classification struggling to remain unclassifiable, is called by the omnibus term surreal, or abstract expressionist, and as we tend to do with anything bizarre or puzzling is referred to the structure of dream—as any play can be. Here the claims for certain types of New Theatre might be looked at askance, for there is another lapse of distinction. What tends to be forgotten—whether we're talking of the dreamlike in old drama or the oneiric in New Theatre—is what Freud never overlooked, that "A dream is in general poorer in affect than the psychical material from the manipulation of which it has proceeded. . . ." It is this material, the *dream-thought*, to which both dreamwork and theatrework are indebted for their staying power, to the extent they really have it. This is another way of saying that whatever the appearances (the manifest content) both play and dream are worlds which in order to appear must first *be thought*.

The play is the thing, but the thing has a history. To make sense of what is happening in the newer theatre—and the relations of performance and drama—we must see it not only as discrete events or separate texts, but as part of a continuum. (A work's inconsequence, seen in the thing itself, is usually due to an absence of such awareness.) The theatrework, like the dream, may be contrued as an increment in the interminable discourse of theatre reflecting historically on itself. I want to emphasize that it is the history of drama, as it has disappeared through representation *in* the theatre, which has insisted on this consciousness. It doesn't disappear because we are disdainful, but because it is self-dispersed. The theatre has always been troubled by its own thought. What we see are the reflected dispersions, or we have not been watching the drama as it has played itself out.

In this sense, the rehearsal process and psychoanalytical process are conflated. I don't mean old-fashioned pseudo-Freudian looking for symbols. The act of interpretation is, rather, an extension of the dream (or pre-text), which is determined by the dream-thoughts as they enter performance. The process of analysis, like the repetitions of rehearsal, attempts to sort them out. Rehearsal is reflection, reflection is rehearsal. When reading a play or making a play, we break down the event or elements, as in dream-analysis, to make them manageable. We come to recognize as we do so that every incident is what Freud calls *over*determined. If there were meanings in the manifest content (or apparent text), meanings accrue *through* the act of interpretation. This includes the presence of an otherness in the acting ensemble, the inevitable mirroring and transference. Each actor is the actor's other. This doubling and splitting figure—like the analyst who mirrors, even in the archetypal silence behind the couch—brings to the play the corporeality of *reflected life* and, with it, the allusive and acrostic self, a product of language. Who's there? The question, and the response, echoes through the thought of performance like the image of Narcissus in the pool.

What theory learns from performance is that we are always interpreting at two major levels, in the seer and the seen. It's as if there were a collision of texts in the collusive occasion—the writing on the page and the inscriptions on the actor's body, coded, genetic, generative, the ghostlier demarcations. It is the writing of history in the fiction of the self, like the strange graffiti on the once "smooth body" of the Ghost, a palimpsest, that self-fathering and self-furthering fiction ("Go on! I'll follow thee.") with which we have, in recent years, become ontologically obsessed. What remains to be seen is how much farther we *can* go. Can the *ghosting* be trusted? Whether it can or not, in my own work that is the name we gave to the process.

It should be clear that almost all the events I have alluded to raise issues of perception or self-perception. They unground both viewer and performance. What is there to be seen and how we see it become the almost ceaseless remainder, *for the time being*, of what is left of the drama, which can't go on (no more than the tramps in *Godot*) without a self-reliable story. That's the reason we're having trouble with the Plot, though it mostly goes on with the reasonable facsimile, which seems like an alibi or an impotency or a lie. We live in a medium of radical discontinuity, in the social world, as in the unconscious. When we look for a stable substance, Heisenberg's principle of indeterminacy backs up the latent content: the instrumentation of the seeing alters the nature of what is seen. Some theatrework directs itself precisely to this process. The reflex of thought mirrors thought until, as Yeats says in a poem, "mirror upon mirror mirrored is all the show." I am not talking about mere relativity of perception from different but stable points of view. The activity of reflection, its reflexiveness, complicates the matter, so that it can't be rationalized. The relativity is ungrounded so that the *relativity is experienced*, not merely as a determinable shifting of points of view, but as the *displacing* and demoralizing thing it is—not the commonplace of modernist thought, but an *opacity* to the source of which one wants to penetrate, like Ahab to the hot heart of the whale.

That was the special undertaking, and maybe vanity, of my own work with the KRAKEN group. The liability is that you will come back with nothing but the opacity; or, like Ahab, sounding and surfacing, wrapped in aspiration around the whale, going under. The structure of the work is meant to be the trace of that sounding. It is the activity of thought pursuing itself through performance. One may see other versions of it, more or less willful, in the self-reflexive activity of some Performance Art (Burden, Montano, Acconci, etc). There is a spoor of association around the memory of a subject which, at the moment of appropriation, seems almost as if it is not-there. Yet *that* is palpable. Wherever one starts—with a text, with history, with random materials, with the apparency of a self—the subject is so thoroughly caught up in the activity of reflection that it virtually disappears into thought, the metamorphic circling of the subject in the self. Is *this* not something more than fantasy? Or therapy? We'll return to that horrid possibility in a moment, though I will be candid now and say that the space of performance borders on a self-cancelling solipsism. Are we self-deceived? Very likely. But if so, it is because we have scrupled much upon the very image of deception, the play within the play of history which, breaking down the old infatuation with substance, beguiles us with appearances. Mirrored in the reflexive logic of theatre, we are brought inevitably to the vanishing subject.

The neurological symptoms of this strange progress are very specific. The condition is like one of those disorders of the brain, called *prosopagnosia*, in which the lesions run fron the underside of the occipital to the temporal lobes on both sides of the cortex. The patient can read, name objects on sight, match images, all other mental functions proceeding unimpaired. He can even identify others by their voices. The one thing that cannot be done is to recognize faces, even those of the closest relatives. The disability is so severe it may even include oneself. And if other voices can be recognized, we're not entirely sure of our own—or that anybody is listening even if it can. But that thought, strangely, is the strongest motive *in* such work, the compulsion to say it and say it even if it can't be heard or (given the untellable story) whether or not we know what it means. "The players cannot keep counsel," says Hamlet, in the echo chamber of the interior play, "they'll tell all."

In recent years there has been, in the most seminal theatre—as if in response to an age of coverup—the disciplined advocacy of confession in acting. There is also the offshoot of explicit autobiography, more or less disciplined, more or less confessed. The best examples are Spalding Gray's Rhode Island trilogy, centered around his mother's suicide, and Lee Breuer's *Animations*, somewhat more elliptical in self-exposure. (We had seen "private moments" in the Method, but this was another order of confession.) Originally, the impulse had something devout about it, a kind of penance, as in the monastic period of Grotowski, who also seized upon the classical Text as a pretext for confession. Now—before this is misunderstood—let's remember that there is a confessional aspect to any great performance, the more fully confessed the more powerful, the more powerful the role the more self-exposure required to fill it. It is not mere authenticity we're talking about either, the self-indulgent spillover of existential sincerity, but a *critical* act as well, *exegetical*, an urgency in the mode of performance (like the trebled insistence of Whitman's procreative Urge Urge Urge), part of its *meaning*, that the Text be *understood*, though the meaning be ever deferred.

That's the more than latent content of the apparently mocking commentary on the inexhaustible play-within-the-play in *Hamlet*. It has all the cruelty of exposure that Freud defines in his essay on wit and the unconscious which, like the Text, is also inexhaustible:

OPHELIA: Will 'a tell us what this show meant?
HAMLET: Ay, or any show that you'll show him. Be not you ashamed to show, he'll not be ashamed to tell you what it means.

But the telling is another meaning, as I've already suggested. Nor are we talking, really, about therapy—what is immediately feared whenever actors or directors dwell upon what is personal about performance with anything more than a surface subjectivity. For some, there is apparently something still scandalous (they call it self-indulgent) about confession. Despite my caution about solipsism, what I have in mind, however, is more like what Marx meant in his essay calling "For a Ruthless Criticism of Everything Existing," where he said that criticism must not be afraid of its own conclusions. The aim is to bring consciousness to the work of the world, clarifying for criticism itself—and I should add, for the theatre—"The meaning of its own struggle and its own desires. . . . It is a matter of confession, no more. To have its sins forgiven mankind has only to declare them to be what they are."

To be perfectly honest and less sanguine than Marx, I'm not even sure about that. But I am not talking about the mere transitory spilling of superficial guts on a vacuous stage, but a lifetime's process of self-understanding in a form which seems to deny the possibility, insisting as it does—the deeper we go into it—that life is a dream. If so, that needs clarification, through performance—the repetition of the Same.

". . . useless;" says Cassandra, "there is no god of healing in this story." Nevertheless, since Freud, you think of dream, you think of therapy. Let me consider now the problematic of therapy in the theatre, for there is undeniably a therapeutic impulse, even where it is minimized or denied, as by me just before, or by Robert Wilson. I'd like to discuss the issue by contrasting what he does in the rather opaque theatre-form he has created, with a more conventional drama, a reasonably good one, Arthur Kopit's play *Wings*. (It may be a way of communicating, for a moment, across the distant worlds of theatre.) Kopit deals dramatically, as Wilson does theatrically, with the subject matter or, in Wilson's case, *subject* of brain damage. I make that distinction because Wilson is notorious for bringing "retarded" or other "disadvantaged" people onto the stage as performers in his work. Some who hear of it think of it as exploitation; some are simply repelled.

His chief collaborator is now Christopher Knowles, who was born seriously aphasic when his mother contracted *toxoplasmosis* (a microscopic parasite) during pregnancy. Knowles was about fifteen when he showed up on stage one evening—actually the opening night of *The Life and Times of Joseph Stalin*—which is the first time most of the other performers had ever seen him. Whatever you feel about Wilson's "use" of such people, what is certain beyond cavil is that he not only discovered the areas in which Chris Knowles is a near-genius (by later aptitude tests) but has also given him, by his parents' grateful testimony, a life about which they never dreamed. Yet Wilson is very insistent that he is not doing therapy. What *is* he doing? Let me put it this way (his extraordinary visual achievements and orchestrations of image aside), just this issue:

In the discourse about structure going on today in, say, literary theory and the social sciences—narrative, mythic, "deep structure"—the essential *difference* (I use the word in deference to Derrida, who makes it the central issue) is between life-determining, if not life-giving or life-supporting, structure, and the construction, however well-intended, which is merely put upon life. Kopit's play is well-intended. It is his most serious play, without the fraternity pledge cleverness of *Oh, Dad, Poor Dad, Mother's Hung You in the Closet and I'm Feelin' So Sad* or the simplistic social criticism of *Indians*, in stride with the adolescent ahistoricism of the sixties. His preface to *Wings*, the play's text, is thoughtful and useful reportage, even moving, as he explains how his father suffered a stroke and eventually died of severe brain damage. While his father was in the hospital, Kopit studied the other patients, their symptoms and behavior, and read up on the nature of brain damage, particularly aphasia.

What was it like inside? he asked himself. He tried to comprehend the structure of brain damage in the writing of the play, creating a character—an older woman who had been an aviator—as a model. But when, in the construction of the drama, it came to getting inside, he reverted in a sense to what was already written, that is, our preconceptions of what it is like inside. He manipulated good observation and invented a language to mimic what he saw. Nobody could doubt the sincerity. But once returned to the mechanisms of the drama—a bourgeois drama after all, with the static regularity of its rhetoric, *that* aphasia, *in* the mechanisms—he was obliged to *make it play*, drawing the reality into a fabricated dramatic climax, as if to redeem the condition by desire, redesigning it as transcendence, inadvertently playing it false.

Now, I realize that Kopit couldn't very well put his dying father on stage—and there is every reason to try to do what he tried to do. It is, however, a respectable play which doesn't quite have the language for what it comes to, and what it comes to can only be transcended *in* language. When at the end the woman dies, it sounds like this: "Oh my, yes, and here it goes then out . . . there I think on . . . wings? Yes . . ." Even in a fine performance, which it apparently had from the actress who played the role, *no*. I forgot. There is a pause and a soft, faint smile: "Thank you."

In Wilson, the structure of brain damage as it enters the structure of performance is another thing altogether, the immanence of another reality, neither an expressive misconstruction nor a mere fiction, but what-it-is, the actuality of another presence displacing the expectancies of performance, and in the estranging language of that presence instituting another mode of discourse. From the outset, Wilson tried to understand the unique vision of the particular aphasia, its interior distance, on the offchance that—as A. R. Ammons says in a poem—"He held radical light/ as music in his skull. . . ." Unlike the therapist admired by Kopit in the hospital and valorized in the play, Wilson did not try to restore Chris Knowles' capacity to think like us, which always raises, as in some mental illness, a subtle ethical question. What he tried to preserve and encourage was the residue of value in the neurological dysfunction—coming up in the process with value unperceived. (Let none of this imply that I am dismissing—no more than I am Kopit's play—the necessary efforts of therapists to keep patients marginally *in* this world.) Wilson has remarked that others who had previously worked with Chris had indeed tried to teach him to speak, hence think, like them. "That was an impossibility," Wilson says. "The child cannot because the brain functions differently, and he will never, never put things together the way we do, because the brain is organized differently. The thought process is different."

Whereupon he enjoined the people in his group to decipher that thought process, to imitate Chris rather than have Chris imitate them. So far this may appear very little different from what Kopit was doing, except that in rehearsal and performance it became a kind of mnemonic learning in the muscles rather than a matter of representation. Chris was there, privileged and dominant. An important space was accorded him in the performance of *Joseph Stalin* which, because there was no telling what he would do with it, since it couldn't be scripted, touched off the resonance of possibility. The structure of subsequent work actually came from Chris, with an imagination, a way of seeing, that would otherwise have been lost—and it was as if he then granted the other actors a reciprocally privileged space in that.

We are asked, then, to follow the aphasic into his own territory, so far as we can think and behave like him, to reverse the normative path of therapeutic imitation, converting the singular dysfunction into a communal energy; an Archimidean point, from which the disadvantage is empowered. Usually, with every ameliorative good wish, we try to bend deformation to our own image of what behavior should be—even the behavior of the deformation. We write plays like that and perform them like that, more often than not. To be fair to Kopit, he does try to imagine what it is to see as the person with the stroke sees, but the liability of the dramatization is that he contrives a structure for it which is a rather romanticized composite, representing not so much the condition as the institutional and ideological version of it. It's hard not to feel (unless you give yourself over to the sentiment, easy enough for some) that, in maintaining the standard kind of authorial control, he not only belies what he cared about but, as with the process of "secondary revision" in the unconscious, he brings it in line with what we already understood before we confronted it. Perhaps it is unavoidable, but in that process there is value lost. You could see it in the concept of the production, at least as described in the text. I can see that such stage effects might be praised, as they were, but the overlay of images, sounds, and transparencies seems to me full of clichés from the remembered theatricality of disjuncture rather than, as with Wilson's visual images, the specificity of *this* rupture of being.

Wilson is of course brilliant in the purest theatrical sense. I would personally quarrel with other aspects of his constituted vision, another kind of opacity than the one I previously invoked—and a quite different attitude toward it. But he has been especially acute, as we see with Chris Knowles, in making available to the theatre what has otherwise been unavailable—and in exchange, making the estranging environment of the theatre of benefit to Chris Knowles, who perhaps finds it natural and familiar as the other world is not. Theatre still remains—despite Chris Knowles' seemingly unmediated presence—something other-than-life, even when, as in Wilson's work, it takes an explicit life to make it so. It is the unfamiliar quality of this life that, alienating the other, contributes to the imposing theatricality of the event.

Wilson requires from his performers (who used to be amateurs, like Chris Knowles; there are now more professionals) other theatrical expectancies, regarding time, motion, role, image, happening and behavior—all of which are returned to the elemental. In that domain, perception seems to occur in other dimensions, with a different rigor, scaled otherwise in time, the movement of a kind of astonishment, going mesmerically to the root of that word. As for Chris Knowles, it seems natural for him to stare into space, unmoving, for hours, or to whirl incessantly, also for hours, like a Sufi dancer; or to arrange whatever it is that *is* thought for him into compulsive geometric patterns (is the sense of compulsion his? ours?) that are as illuminating as cave drawings or an art read, at the other end of time's spectrum of apparencies, from computer printouts. In all this, there is a differentiating intelligence that was previously overlooked. The boy's father reports how conventional psychologists misjudged his tests, not knowing what to make of those scores in which he exceeded anything they could anticipate, as if he'd seen the questions or cheated.

That's the way some people appraise new things in the theatre, as if there were cheating going on. Well, maybe the whole thing is a hoax. (Plato thought so.) "YOU KNOW WHAT I'M SAYING ." In some new work turning on solipsism—like Bill Raymond (of the Mabou Mines) attached to his puppet in a double telephone booth—we also try to get that suspicion into the form. At the returning end of the circling dodge of the oedipal story, we come to the pained parody of *The Shaggy Dog*: "WHAT CAN I DO . I GO INTO MYSELF . I BECOME SELF INVOLVED . I TRY TO BE SELF EFFACING . BUT THAT'S SELF DEFEATING . I INDULGE IN SELF RECRIMINATION . BUT ALL THAT DOES IS MAKE ME MORE SELF CENTERED . I LONG TO BE SELF TRANSCENDING . WHICH BRINGS ME TO THE BRINK OF SELF DESTRUCTION . WHICH BECOMES A SUBJECT OF SELF CONCERN . AM I BEING SELF INDULGENT . GOOD . GOOD . JUST CHECKING ."

What is true of some newer forms of theatre is more or less true of all theatre. The point is, however, that it is *more* true, and more self-consciously true of newer theatre, in which the play-within-the-play is now a convention so thoroughly absorbed into the tradition as to demoralize our definitions of a play. Since Pirandello, the self-reflexivity of play has become, as I have suggested, both the subject matter and the articulating mechanism of performance, the very instrument of analysis in the enactment, its subject. In this respect, we are reminded that the structure of a play is a correlative of the structure of dream, with its processes of condensation, substitution and displacement, representability, and secondary revision. These processes are so powerful, so doubled over by the revisionism of history, in dream, in theatre, that they even absorb the act of interpretation. I mean we have to reconsider what we mean by interpretation, as analysis itself is caught up in the structure. It is within this perspective of theatre that the work I have been doing over the last decade has been done. In everything from methodology of inquiry to the act of performance, the energy of the work comes from the effort to interpret the subject as it is being performed, performing the interpretation.

There are subsidiary issues: like the deconstructed character or displaced person over which the theatre had been worrying since the Author seemed to get lost. The dematerializing character is a function of the disappearing subject which we have tried to make the basis of a reconstruction of the acting process. What we are dealing with in such work is the ordination of acting possibilities on a scale of conceivable behaviors, what you might think of as a palette of concepts or gradients of identity: self person actor role persona mask mirror double shadow and the *memory* of character, allusions to it, brushstrokes of presence, *intimations*, and then these concepts being played against each other, hues, colors, configurations, as if they were a language, as they are.

It is this language, or spectrum of behaviors, that we were experimenting with in *The Donner Party, Its Crossing*. The roles which appear to be there are not-quite, neither assigned, transformed, nor exchanged sequentially, now one, now another, but essentially playing a role, even if fractured; rather, the historical persons named are more like *latencies*, now suggested, elicited, invoked, alluded to, momentarily played out, quoted, in the passage through a landscape of a text evolved in the crossing (structure, subject, idea of acting), where nobody is exempt from any line of the discourse (not-quite-dialogue), every line being the subtext or fantasy text of every other line, no matter who speaks it, as if there were one surviving voice in the shattered unity of collective behavior which, even before the eating at Donner Pass, is the cannibalism in the crossing, *that* subject.

The Donner Party, Its Crossing is presumably about the migrants who went to California in 1846, at the time of the Mexican War, only to be snowbound in the Sierras after being devastated in the desert, and did what they had to do, those who survived. There is only the trace of a narrative in the structure. What it is, instead, is a network of speculation around one of those unassimilated remnants of American history which seems on reflection like some originary pollution. Every inch of territory settled has some memory like that, almost better forgotten, like abandoned stripmines or the sewage spill that has just made a virtual septic tank of the southern tip of San Francisco Bay. It "is now a zone of total mortality," says the Fish and Game Department. "Nothing is alive." So it must also have seemed once to the volitionless consciousness of snow as it settled massively over those dismembered bodies. *Where were they going?*

That was the retrospective question explored by the work and specifically asked of the actors (about whom the play *is*, who else is there?) through more than a year of rehearsal. And the correlative questions, both historical and immediate: *What does it mean to get over the Donner Pass?* and what does it mean to fail? It's not so much that these questions are answerable (nor that such a work can even be accomplished), but that there was in the work, as it developed, something like a monomania of will and mind to attempt an answer, at the opacity of the Pass, *in* the performance *by means of* performance—which is not the realization of a prior text already formulated, but a text discovered, so far as it exists in the inscription of history, *through* the crossing, like a judgment of the muscles. The whole thing is done from beginning to end in the ceaseless callings of a square dance, the whirling figures of the dance reflecting the cross-currents of perception, wheel upon turning wheel, still turning as they are buried in their cabins twenty feet beneath the snow, both minds and bodies exhausted in the elliptical telling of a story that—like a lesion of memory below the temporal lobes—cannot conceivably be told.

Or in *Elsinore*, which was derived from the *memory* of *Hamlet* in a crossfire of reflexions, there is no character of Hamlet, nor any perceivable sequencing of the lineaments of a role. What there seems to be, in the ghosting process of performance, is a piece of him, shadows and reflections, figures conjectures affects affinities double exposures, as if Hamlet were the *thought* of Ophelia or the *aura* of Claudius, an abstract and brief chronicle of a differential self, nothing sufficiently whole or legibly still for more than the illusion of a nominal moment. Rather, if you were to ask, where's Hamlet? you'd be referred by the multiple exposures of ideographic space, laminated, to the whole distributed presence of performance, as if Hamlet—neither character nor role nor person nor actor, but *a suffusing presence like thought*—were an anamorphic energy in the air, dreamwork, inexhaustibly elusive and endlessly interpretable, like the sounding specificity of that brain-damaged site whose name is Elsinore, or the vanishing subject in the hemorrhage of history, actual, immanent, equivocally there, dream-thought.

The Remission of Play

●

"We had lost all pleasure in this game of chase, and we weren't children any more for that matter, but now there was nothing else we could do."

Italo Calvino, "Games Without End," *Cosmicomics*

SINCE THE RADICAL IMPULSE OF PERFORMANCE IS INHERENTLY REACtionary—dancing back the tribal morn or, like Artaud's actor, signalling through the flames—I am somewhat embarrassed to say that my own concern for innovation arose from less ecstatic progressive tendencies in our liberal tradition. My convictions about the theatre were formed in a period when the prospect of a repertory theatre with *continuity*—a cultural rarity in the United States—seemed an aspect of the emerging struggle for Civil Rights. Through the political inertia of the fifties, in the first fallout over the Bomb, it was necessary to revive a case (it had actually been made in the thirties but dismantled as "creeping socialism") for the relevance of theatre to society. It's something you appear to take for granted, with whatever grievances, in England, France or Germany, and in societies where the theatre seems even more naturally grounded, as in Bali or Senegal, performance is both aboriginal *and* contemporary, and innovation seemed irrelevant until the dancers came out of the bush to go on tour, and the attritions of world travel, with thousands of curious eyes, started to adulterate those seemingly Eternal Forms. So, to begin with, the issues of innovation or renovation in performance are relative to where you are, historically, and what sort of continuity you have.

In America, it wasn't until they started to think the unthinkable in the Pentagon that we started to think about permanence in the theatre. The radical thing was survival, in both theatre and society, but activism was—as Winnie says of love in Beckett's *Happy Days*—in "the old style," and experiment was tentative—with a little *Verfremdungseffekt* and increasing dosages of the Absurd—until all continuity was disrupted in the sixties, when reality took on the character of a performance. As the dissidence thickened with the unthinkable, it was soon something of a non sequitur to ask whether the theatre is relevant to society, but whether—in a world of pseudo-image and after-image, identity crises and new life-styles, demonstrations and Happenings, role-models and play therapy, the improvising of confrontations and the staging of coverups, as well as the convergence of the Biomedical Revolution with the *mise en scène* of the Unconscious and other cybernetic fantasies, like the play-within-the-play, feedback and freakouts, transplants (the first one, by the way, reversing Clytemnestra, a woman's heart in a male body) and transformations: genetic management, doctored sound, permutated sex and programmed dreams—we were really getting the message of the media (Deep-Throated and beamed by satellite), that society may be nothing but a scenario after all, with Total Theatre at the living end.

Over the global village falls the veil of Maya. Amazement sits upon the brow. We are not only talking about play, but in the galaxy of the Imaginary the immanence of World-Play. If we follow the play of thought—the whole planet thoroughly imaged—we encounter a paradox: through the shimmering display of signs, we are in the service of the imageless. The play of surface is the measure of an invisible exchange. There are eyes everywhere. What we now call spectacle is the reflex of surveillance. The world that was a stage—even the old two boards and a passion—seems to have been deconstructed and whittled into the world. There is nothing that we see, not a single gesture made in the psychopathology of everyday life, which is not an assignation with an invisible power. This is doubly true of the theatre doubling upon itself and unsuspectingly in the service of what it reveals. It is an array of inquisitive mechanisms put into operation by the ingenuously self-seeking Oedipus, the instruments of a vast apparatus of surveillance—as in the scabrously mirrored fantasies of Genet's brothel, an almost demonic structure of watching and being watched—of which the CIA and the SAVAK and the GPU are merely the top not the bottom of the iceberg; or, as Genet would have it, the mausoleum, in which the Police Chief would be reflected to infinity.

The rest is less magnificent and more insidious because part of the documentation of everyday life and the "docudrama" of historical life in which, as Shakespeare had warned in *Measure for Measure*, "millions of false eyes/ Are stuck upon thee; volumes of report/ Run with these false": on every bill we pay, every breath we breathe, procedures, records, traces, verifications, puchcard lines of force, and a whole relational system of surrendered power in which—as Michel Foucault repeatedly points out—far from being denied individuality, we are granted it outright, by number, status, code, file; signed, sealed and delivered to our distinction.

When, during the Vietnam War, the delivery system became demonic, some were scared to death and simply took to the hills; or, in that homeopathic magic whereby conspiracy subverts conspiracy, went underground, with lethal consequences we saw later in Europe, in the Red Guards or the Baader-Meinhof group, and aesthetic consequences, such as the nomadic paranoia of The Living Theater or the para-sitical homesteading of the Hungarian group Squat, which is living now and performing in the United States. It seemed a kind of poetic destiny and part of the conspiratorial pattern when, in 1979, the documentation of the outlawed performances given by Squat in their apartment in Budapest was destroyed by a fire in their storefront theatre in New York. The members of the company—acquisitive as squatters in their survival techniques—say with arch irony that "they highly appreciate happenings 'by accident' "; they seem to like the idea of only partially readable remnants of their past, like the charred palimpsest of a legend, which "give some meaning, some sense, of that time."

Now they develop pieces for our time out of an obsessional personal mythology in a Pop-porno-Surrealist form which is the ritualized liminal outgrowth of the life they collectively live, which may—in one of their recent works—be watched through the plate glass window. Sometimes, their lives may spill out onto the street, where they may even pick up performers from among the indigents passing by, in a catatonic parody of social identity, the dubious achievement of which remains—through the equivocal narcissism, a tradition of shock tactics, and a surfeit of indeterminate play—the unsettling recidivist mission of the postmodern, and a major source of innovation.

Like the Théâtre du Soleil—a post-Brechtian collective born in Paris of the Days of May—Squat is a further mutation of the communitarian anarchy of the sixties. The activities in their works have ranged from washing the dishes and taking care of the baby (who was almost born on stage, and symbolically knifed), to transvestitism and vein-cutting, and the politically saturated sequence in which a dwarf uses Zen archery to combat King Kong who—before his phallus is bloodily ripped out by a New York vamp—responds to the attack with quotations from Blake's "Proverbs of Hell." After an early phase of avant-garde self-inquiry, the work of the Théâtre du Soleil was determined to be less in-

sular and more legible, and more specifically historical—though posi-
tioning itself as far as possible outside the conventional theatre system.
The production of *1789*—subtitled *The Revolution Must Continue to
the Perfection of Happiness*—was performed in an abandoned muni-
tions factory in a suburb of Paris, where the crowds were moved
around with giant puppets as at a carnival, or at one of Robespierre's
pageants as it might have been staged by a proletarianized David.

It is a work of considerable scale as compared to that of Squat
which—for all its exhibitionism—is more furtive, self-enveloped and
encoded. As older politicized groups disappear, Squat is now part of a
growing circuit of "private" and "solo" performances extending—sometimes arcane, sometimes ribald with political residues, like
a fusion of *Samizdat*, Gurdjieff, Joseph Beuys and Lenny Bruce—all
the way from lower Manhattan across the Atlantic Alliance through
unaligned Europe to the Theater on Chekov Street, where young actors
brought up on Stanislavski are performing clandestine "rituals" which
might have been staged by Grotowski, who is currently seeking liberation (about which, more later) by retreating to the Source.

While the more desublimated illusions of liberation, abraded by
politics, seem to be in hiding, our concepts of performance,
(re)sublimated in theory, are still modulating or consolidating the
liturgy of the sixties. First of all, the primacy of the *staging*, dominion
of the performance itself. Datum: subversion of the authoritarian Text
and the system of ideological support. As the demonstrators said in the
charges against Jean Vilar at Avignon in 1968, when The Living
Theater was forbidden to perform in the Cour des Papes, the theatre
must be freed "from the censure that annuls it" as "the unconscious is
liberated from the regime that negates it." Behind that insistence was a
view of the actor's old relationship to the Text as a form of servitude or
a Faustian pact, in either case the actor conceding the autonomy of his
body to the exigencies of the Text in exchange for the illusion, to the
spectator, that the *character* being played is real. That is a social con-
tract with an ideological subtext inscribed, as the feminists now say, in
the Name of the Father, with all the vertical articulations of power in
that formerly resistless and invaginated Name.

When I came into the theatre that was orthodoxy. We used to speak,
as if it were gospel, about being "faithful" to the Text, *"line perfect,"*
doing "what the playwright wants," which was very rarely questioned,
and then only with the finest discretion about a variation. When the
playwright was not present or dead what he wanted was a problem,
but *that*—the actors were always told (I told them myself)—was apparent in the Text. In the European theatre this allegiance to the Text
had its institutional embodiments, like the Comédie Française, which

at the time we envied, though it entailed a servitude to the classics displayed to which there could be no equivalent in the United States, where we were as a result even more slavish to the idea that the final arbiter of all desire in the act of interpretation was (as in the New Criticism) the indelible word on the page.

After Brecht, we started to ask whether the actor—that former ventriloquist's dummy—could *agree* with the words; if not, he might strike that part of the Text as an assumption of freedom. Abruptly, we turned the Stanislavski Superobjective upside down, like Marx turned Hegel, asking not what the character wants but what the actor wants, however blasphemous to the Text. The blasphemy was intensified by Artaud, whipping his "innateness," and passing it on to the actor, while reasserting the imperial claim of the Director, with the *mise en scène* emerging as a nearly autonomous force. In that process, the staging was to be a transgression of the Symbolic (in the Lacanian sense), an erotics of performance (in Barthes' sense), an infinitely curving field of parabolic play, further disempowering an already disappearing Origin; and there are presently young directors in France, like Mesguich or Gourville, who think like Althusser or sound like Derrida. The philosophical intricacy of Derrida—the arcanum and transparency of the "Writing before the Letter"—was synchronously spelled out in their studio exercises by the intervolving bodies of American actors in their uncontrollable mysteries on the bestial floor, and *literally* by The Living Theater in the corporeal writing of *Paradise Now*. Simpleminded as some of them were, those "psychophysical" exercises—along with the occultations of the Counter-Culture—turned on the Europeans, who have been busy ever since giving them intellectual dimension, fortified by all the theoretical depredations on the signifying Word.

While there was a (sluggish) restoration of the Word onstage during the decade that followed, there are still repercussions of that short-circuiting of the normal conduits of discourse, whose power is invested in the invisible. In short, who had the power? and where was it situated? and if it couldn't be discerned, then *displacement* would become the strategy of innovation, if only in self-protection. Performance would move out of the duplicitous "privileged space" into other arts and other disciplines, which were meanwhile using theatre to disenfranchise themselves. Secular prey to the specular, the old laws of theatre were dematerialized into the unruly speculations of a shifting subject, which performs by echolocation. If it sometimes resembled the action of urban guerrillas with scrambled walkie-talkies, it was also the manifest destiny of subversion *within* the historical evolution of the form. One can imagine the gasman Antoine in the Théâtre Libre transformed into Genet's gasman in the brothel by way of Jarry's debraining machine and Pirandello's *Six Characters in Search of an Author*, who were in turn divided up by Brecht's Alienation and broken down by Artaud's Alchemy, with its "unremitting pulverization of every insufficiently fine, insufficiently matured form . . . through all the filters and foundations of existing matter" into an almost onomotopoeic alphabet of physiological signs.

This apocalyptic radicalization came out of the almost compulsive historical assault on *representation*. The theatre was asking not only *what* was being represented but *who* was doing the representing and by what suspect means. That in part accounts for the shift away not only from the established theatres but from the word/idea of theatre itself to the idea of *performance*. For there is no way to resolve what theatre is, a *sui generis* event or a tautologous representation of something other than what it appears to be. That it *appears* to be, or in *order* to be, is one of its troubling aspects, even when—with non-theatrical candor—it is denying representation by the representation of its own denial; no matter what, a representation representing itself either *as* itself or something other, with infinite combinatorial possibilities for that other, making for degrees and inversions of illusion, as well as renewals of the age-long desire to abolish it.

Cross-eyed representation: the problem is that it is somehow bisected in its *appearance* by what the American Method actor, with a heavy psychological bias, dismisses as *indication* (or untruth), forgetting that he is inevitably indicating what *that* psychology—a compound of oblique Skinnerism and popular Freudianism—prescribes (as truth); just as the eighteenth century—drawing on a faculty psychology going back to the Ancients—designated (as truth), the precise indication of appearance, apparently as prescribed in its articulations (with Garrick or Betterton) as the *mudras* or eye-rollings of the Kathakali, which had an *un*inhibiting influence on our ideas of acting over the last generation. The running argument in acting about indication is an argument—going back to Diderot and Delsarte even before Saussure—about the arbitrariness of the sign. To anyone in the theatre who thinks about it, Structuralism is a high theorization of the discourse on acting, as we can see (though his theory of discursive practice rejects the label Structuralism) in Foucault's remark that representation is, "in its peculiar essence always perpendicular to itself: it is at the same time *indication* and *appearance*; a relation to an object and a manifestation of itself. From the Classical age, the sign is the representativity of the representation in so far as it is *representable*." And in so far as it is representable, there is potentially the high melodrama of complicity that Derrida (in a quite Augustinian way) warns against, the promiscuous and illicit redundancy of reflections which deny reference and disperse origins in the narcissistic reflecting pool—like the "private moment" of the old Method actor, like Marlon Brando in the Studio, or the equally private moment of the newer Conceptual Artist, like Vito Acconci in *Seedbed*, who is not only on the bestial floor but regressively *under* it, masturbating over an amplifier. *Last Tango in Paris* is the French connection.

In the spilled seed, still-breeding thought: in the unwatched eye, the look of something that is looked at: speculation doubling and braided, expelling all thought of identity since, as Derrida reminds us, "What can look at itself is not one. . . ." And the noise which comes over the amplifier is an insufferable static, like the voiced ubiquity of repressed history, which sticks in the thorax like velcro. Which gives some justification to the redundancy, since we know from cybernetic theory, as from post-serial music, that redundancy is required in a system to get through the noise, which is most deeply perceived in silence. No wonder, then, that performance went, with all the public outburst, non-verbal or anti-verbal or spastically verbal for a while: or flooded like a burst bloodvessel of engorged thought into a logorrhea of abuse, as in Peter Handke's *Offending the Audience*, in which we also feel the self-mocking babel of the actor's double bind as he tries to get out from under the false bottom of mimesis, by not-performing, and the falsifying pathos of fictive time, where something was always happening which tries to hide and expose itself at on(c)e, as if there were no eyewitness to the event which never occurred until *now*, a perpetual present moment which he knows is all a *pretense*.

The break with established discourse and the extension of theatre into other conceptual space led to a reconstrual *in* the theatre of every aspect of performance: subject matter and subject, language, audience, playing space and duration, play itself, techniques of production (against the "production ethic" and in the spirit of *bricolage*, not productions but "pieces," "events," "activities"), operational principles in a troupe, questions of ownership and property, amateurism or expertise?, in the disputed provenance of the Text the issue of a presiding presence, problems of depth and surface, duplicity and doubleness, imitation and metathesis (in the uninterrupted middle, the question of beginnings and ends), the acting body and the Body Politic, the issue of participation and the nature of power (restoring production with the repossessed means), the conduct of rehearsal (Fr., *répétition*: in the confusions of anamnesis, the dangers of the returning Same), acting methodology, improvisational form, standards of credibility (as inscribed on the price of the ticket, or with no tickets at all), scale and privacy, confession, the disappearance of the Chorus in the murmur of history, the "deep structure" of voice (*sounding*: the original plenitude and the phōne), ideographical or behavioral notation, theatre as therapy, or ritualization, masking, solipsism, "Seeming, seeming" and polyseming, *theatricality* itself as it seems irremediably attached to representation, and thus subject to obscurantism (curtains? screening? tormentors? teasers? white light?), the illusion that sustains the discourse that, *in appearance*, seems to be exposed.

There was also serious thought for a while—in France (with the shaken but durable presence of the Comédie) and in Germany (with its heritage of State theatres) and in England (with no intention of giving up Shakespeaare to the Germans, who think they own him)—to the place reserved for *tradition* and for the institution of theatre in society. This was, as I've suggested, not a question that could really be debated in America, where the theatre was belatedly spawned in an anti-intellectual atmosphere of no-theory which persists to this day, and there is no similar tradition to protect. *La mise en pièce et contestation du Cid*, a "collective creation" under the guidance of Planchon, addressed itself to this issue in 1968, and the debate continues about the Centres Dramatiques. For a while, as in the animosities surrounding Gunter Grass' dialectical assault on Brecht, another question had to be entertained: why bother, as in *Le Cid* or The Berliner Ensemble's *Coriolanus*, with fake fighting on stage when there are pitched battles in the streets?

We may think the question has disappeared with guerrilla theatre, but it is revived anywhere in the world where an insurrection arises, as in Columbia, and Americans have an almost absurdly peculiar perspective on it right now, as we watch the weird proceedings in Iran through images provided by our own television cameras, while German actors read from the stage a letter from Gunter Grass to Chancellor Schmidt asking for a break with American foreign policy. Innovation in Iran or Rhodesia or Nicaragua is, even when the fighting stops, an altogether different affair; and we haven't yet heard of experimental theatre activity in Cuba, certainly not of the formalist kind (the Bolshevik Revolution ended that with Meyerhold), though it may be sufficiently innovative in some parts of the world to bring theatre of the simplest kind to people who've never seen it. Or, as Peter Brook and Eugenio Barba have done, used such expeditions as a possible pretext for a later formalism, in Brook's case with a polyglot group of carefully chosen performers who speak in their separate languages to people who don't understand the words at all.

That a sort of world community might be achieved by means of theatre—by rolling out a carpet in an African village or performing on a raft down the Mississippi or by immemorial incantations in the air over Persepolis, crossing the barriers of culture and time—is a notion which still has some currency against and within that other tide, the closure of representation, or the eddies of small voices distributed in solo performances all over the world, some of them (coming up from the Gulag) barely making a sound at all. For the distance between underground performances is as great as that between a maximum security prison and Broadway or between Soho and Moscow, never mind Persepolis (where Brook's *Orghast*, drawing on *Life Is a Dream* in the language of Zoroaster, was financed by the Shah). When the Theater on Chekov Street does a ceremony in which a live carp is cut apart and cooked in a congested space with no ventilation for the smoking oil, the high solemnity and the political risk rise in the inhalations as they simply do not in the lofts, bistros, and apartments of lower Broadway, where fellow artists perform for each other and congenial visitors, with more or less paranoia or solipsism, but little secrecy—and ambivalent feelings about *not* being watched.

Assessing the scattered energies of innovation after the sixties, Julia Kristeva wrote in 1977: "Modern theatre does not exist—it does not take (a) place—and consequently its semiology is a mirage." As we might also expect, Kristeva argues that the theatre does not exist outside a Text, so what we are dealing with is not so much a failure of representation but of *demonstration* (or, to lend a reproachful piety to the showing, a *remonstrance*), as if, like Othello, the theatre wants ocular proof of the existence of a communal discourse for play which, if it existed, we would reject, since it would be supported by the Sacred, in which we cannot believe without the mirage. Without the Sacred, a communal discourse is for all profane purposes insupportable. What's left? only private fantasies, as Mallarmé predicted. The withdrawal of the Sacred into language made it possible to sustain fantasies for private consciousness—assuring the theatre of a public of *one*, but *one divided*, as we've seen, that audience enlarged by the exponential fractures of Original Division, as in the solo performance of the broken King Richard in Pomfret Castle.

Kristeva is not the only one who believes that every attempt by an avant-garde to reconstitute a space of play for collective representation is necessarily illusory or short-lived, and more or less evasive of the central issue: that if a space of theatre were to exist at all within the supersaturated spectacle of World-Play, it would be in displaced and imaginary circles of individual consciousness, where no-time *is*, as in the *mise en scène* of the Unconscious. The liability of the contracting circle, contracting the actor to his own bright eye, is that performance may just barely exist, or not at all, in the objective world, and only as a vanishing into thought, the nature of performance becoming the destiny of performance. (Exactly this possibility was the *subject* of my own work with the KRAKEN group, putting the liability aside.) Or it might regress in another direction and attach itself to *things*, like the string tying an actor or an orange to a chair, coequally, in the theory behind the "landscape plays" of Richard Foreman. The actual landscape of his Ontological-Hysteric Theater is indebted (and the term) to Gertrude Stein; and like her prose it is a species of performance which thinks of itself *as thought*, but *beginning all over again*, which seems to be—with every de-definition of art—what innovation has become. But there are definitions to be made within the de-definitions:

Foreman is one of those who has wanted to drain out of play the old *expressivity* of the drama. His theatre pieces are like an exegesis in motion of the phenomenological reduction of Minimalist art, cooled down originally by an affinity with Brecht. In the semiotic atmosphere of the human sciences, Foreman has been admired in Europe for these clinically surreal and cerebral plays, which he virtually conducts from the lighting console, barking out cues and blowing the whistle for changes in tempo, as the actors go through a disjunct puppetry of acutely choreographed paces on a stage rigged out like a Chinese puzzle box. Foreman's manifestoes are somewhat cribbed from Merleau-Ponty, but the performances—like the umbrella and sewing-machine on the surgical table—are nothing like a phenomenology of the body. As with certain forms of contemporary dance, or the more gregarious pageants of the Bread and Puppet Theater, almost anybody can perform in one of these plays, though certain actors are by now identified with them. The more rigorous training of the body in the sixties left us, however, with a reservoir of actors who would be put off by the slapstick asepsis of such a form. They are not only able to take physical risks we could never have asked of actors a generation before, but they can also *think* ideographically and insist on doing so, as if it were "a matter of *confession*, no more," as Marx put it in his letter to Dr. Ruge calling for the *"ruthless criticism of everything existing. . . ."*

In the obsession with "body language"in the sixties, there was, however, an almost purely uncognitive phase where the theatre seemed to be groping toward a primal unity with dance. Much of the groping—olfactory exercises, touch therapy, and ass-to-mouth connections—was rather brainless, only suggesting in the effort to break down the "mental hangups" of God's frozen people that there is a limited wisdom in the unlocked body. We used to think of dancers as brainless too, but when dance began to think, after Martha Graham, it eventually did so with a vengeance. "I don't have ideas, exactly," said the elliptical Merce Cunningham, who gave plenty of ideas to Yvonne Rainer, who once did a piece named, as if from Nietzsche, *The Mind Is a Muscle*. "If my rage at the impoverishment of ideas, narcissism, and disguised sexual exhibitionism of most dancing can be considered puritan moralizing," she wrote in the program (1968), "it is also true I love the body—its actual weight, mass, and unenhanced physicality."

What Rainer said of dancers could also have been said of actors of the period, as Grotowski soon did of his American imitators. Her love of the body was, even when most abandoned, more conceptualized. *The Mind Is a Muscle* was a theory in performance, strenuously un-mimetic and encapsulated: the dancers never even gazed at the audience in order to avert the solicitations of performance—its "problem," wanting empathy—in favor of commensurate motion, equilibrated to *task* or *movement-as-object*. (The Open Theater's gamesmanship, qualified by Stanslavski's method of physical actions, also emphasized tasks, but with a more psychological orientation.) The labor input is not disguised but registered. You are supposed to see the dancers sweat. So with Grotowski's actors, but for more existential, confessional, less minimalist reasons.

Still, Rainer's performance-*work* has always had an autobiographical base. But it was, in one of the registers of the time (as with Foreman), cannily or wittily distanced, on a wobbling pivot between the severest of tasks, *like* formal requirements, and a sort of ex-hilarating free play, as a decoy for constructed fictions. (I once saw her break arbitrarily from an improvising ensemble and walk a manic gleam of hallucinatory purpose over the heads of the audience.) These fictions, as in *Lives of Performers*, became more openly feminist and, abandoning dance, are now being choreographed into film. This shift is personal and more widely symptomatic, reflecting not only upon Rainer's career in and beyond dance, which has never been much for politics, but upon the theatre, where the depletion of politics has been held responsible, as in a recent article by Richard Schechner [*Performing Arts Journal*, Nos. 14 & 15] for the current bleakness of the avant-garde.

The Mind Is a Muscle was performed with the Vietnam atrocities on her mind, but Rainer insisted then that ideological issues had no bearing on the work, which nevertheless felt "tenuous and remote" from the world crisis. The body was still "the enduring reality," but she could foresee a time when the remoteness had to end, as it has been doing through the withdrawal of the body into the cinematic image—with its paradoxical impression of immediacy. Very recently—during the filming of *Journeys to Berlin/1971*—she was living in West Berlin and had direct contact with victims of surveillance. Aroused by the climate, and language, of repression written into law—in reaction to the Baader-Meinhof violence—she revised the end of her film to put on record what the head of the BKA called "*the State's monopoly of force.*" She was careful to indicate, remembering repression at home—as well as the "gentle *semiurgy*" (Jean

Baudrillard) of "friendly fascism" (Bertram Gross) throughout the in-
dustrialized world—that it is not only Germany that concerns her.

It is not irrelevant, however, that the film happens to have been
done in Germany, with its mixture of political stability, affluence, and
paranoia supporting a renaissance of experimental film-making, along
with the considerable dissidence in its state-supported theatres, about
the limits of which I shall say more in a moment. In Germany, there is
a stimulating cross-fertilization of film and theatre, with the same
distinguished actors performing in both, and sometimes in very experimental work, as Klaus Kinski does with Werner Herzog, or Heinz
Schubert with Hans-Jurgen Syberberg. The situation is very different
in America, where a superstar might be induced to ballast a Broadway
play, but where you wouldn't expect anybody of that status to take any
further risk. As the power of the cinematic industry has grown, it has
appropriated powerful energies of performance and most of the major
talent that might once have been in the theatre, where the devalued
dollar is not so available nor, even for people of some reputation, jobs.
As for women artists of Rainer's status, turning to film is, politically,
the first step toward expropriating the expropriators who control the
image repertoire and, psychically, like following the thread back to the
Minotaur. There are numerous feminist theatre and dance collectives,
but film is the lair of feminist theory, with its assault on phallocentrism
and the much-belabored doxy of presence-as-absence, projected in the
female Body-as-Object.

Most dance, however, continues in Europe and America, with
whatever feminist impulses, in the other apolitical tradition. The
tenuous distance between the two is a possible measure of what you
take to be innovative. That's one of the conclusions being drawn about
the state of innovation in our theatre. But there's a chastening irony. If
where you are politically determines how innovative you may be,
where you are geographically determines how political you may
be—and with that, either a loss of effectiveness because of too much
tolerance, or a gain of longevity for what would not, as art or politics,
seem as urgent as it once was. We see that with Squat in New York and
with The Living Theater in Rome. It leaves something to be desired in
our theorizing about the relationship of innovation and politics, which
is also a matter of timing, the placement of art in history, which also
makes judgments for the wrong reasons. Or, past the best of reasons,
reasons not at all:

"Brecht sang:" writes Augusto Boal at the end of his book on *Theater
of the Oppressed*, " 'Happy is the people who needs no heroes.' I agree.
But we are not a happy people: for this reason we need heroes." Boal's
theatre was surely innovative in Sao Paulo, where I suppose The Living
Theater was too, before they were incarcerated, although the objective

conditions for its revolutionary aspirations no longer existed, if they ever did, in the United States. We are not a happy people, but I'm not sure we need heroes, or if we do, what kind of heroes they should be. The problem remains that for certain politicized intensities in the theatre we require a historical situation that endorses a kind of binary thinking, even if it's anthropologized, as with Schechner (who knows better), or mythicized, as with The Living Theater.

When, however, Orpheus evokes Prometheus at the storming of the Winter Palace, we are in another country, and besides the wench is dead, Isadora, *"ready for a new myth/ since the Bolshevik one didn't turn out. . . ."* Before that admission, Lenin/Julian Beck arouses the audience to participate as Red Guards, People's Brigade, Narodniks, Terrorists, Anarchists, Women, and Tolstoyan Pacifists, etc. In having to "face once again," in their recent collective creation *Prometheus, "all the issues/ which have been with the Living Theater/ since the very beginning,"* we see how far that heroic group is from being able to face them in America, now, with any ideological complexity, not to mention persuasive power. "Theatre ought to be," says Schechner, "and can be, as important to people as the price of hamburger." For the people in the more advantaged countries, I seriously doubt it, since the price of hamburger is so variously important, and will be in the negotiable future. If there's *"an end to words deeds/ now,"* the innovation seems to be coming, in American politics, from the New Conservatism; and to the degree we've had it in the theatre, it's from a new aestheticism or solipsism. If there's a kind of poetic justice in the fact that the operatic costs of Robert Wilson's elitism are accomodated at the Met or in West Berlin, the city of Aphasia, where the apolitical non sequiturs of the Knee Plays run into the indubitable Wall, so it seems right that The Living Theater's anarchism, still pressing its *"hand against/ eternity,"* is embraced by Autonomia in the city of the Sistine Ceiling, where a kneecap is still likely to be shot off.

But to return through the shin splints of ideology for one last reflection on an art which can't sustain a politics and has been trying in recent years to minimize the aesthetics too. The rhetoric of the New Dance has had its impact on the theatre, and it is now as susceptible to definition as the paradigmatic dance it displaced: unencoded and quotidian movement, with maybe a parodistic obeisance to the broken barre and the remembered step; if things are there, there sparsely, no impediment to the body's presence; the music arising (via Cage's noise) from the order of Silence, in the spaces between—the frequencies of discovered sound or the scansion of randomly or serially moving feet; separate, additive, cyclical or reversed. Reservations, of course, about the degree of randomness, as with Meredith Monk, who has also wanted a more *expressive* theatricalized space, refusing to leave things to chance. "John Cage would say there's enough structure and I would say there's enough chance." Most companies now take their chances with structure, but among the many techniques the aleatoric astringency of Cunningham's is dominant. Even when everyday occurrences are explored for emotional content, as by Pina Bausch in provincial Wuppertal, it is within the *Zeitgeist* of *indeterminacy* which possesses the arts and literature in the era of the postmodern. Along with the disjunct reflexions of the untellable tale and the splitting subject, there is a theodicy of *interruption* and the sovereignty of *the recursive principle*—all of which has political implications if it doesn't constitute a politics.

The repetitions of rehearsal, like the *vers libre* which is not *vers*, have always had to do with the *measuring* of redundancy. In the old dramaturgy, we always worried about how long and repetitive the behavior of a scene should be, as appearances kept slipping away. Has the audience seen *enough*? Enough for *what*? What I once learned as simple timing turned out to be a metaphysic in a time-serving form, as the system transposes gestures, words, happenings, thought in the rhythmic interplay through space of light, sound, color, and behavior, human and otherwise. In the conventional system of drama, there was the calculated deterioration of forms, the metonymies of representation. But in *Einstein on the Beach*, Robert Wilson plays with a sort of particle physics of that problem, including the long slow petrification of motion in high-energy states. In over two hours of repetition the first two letters of the alphabet become a code which, once established, can be permutated for several hours more. But the question remains: how long do the repetitions need to occur before the code is established? In the alternations of order and disorder within the structure of a work, or within an artistic tradition, the issue becomes one of controlling what, to use Robbe-Grillet's term, one may think of as *slippages*, the displaced continuity of decentralizations: "It is never a question of replacing the Tsar's statue," says Robbe-Grillet, "by a statue of Stalin. It is a question of never placing any statue in position, but continuing to slip." The unexpected outcome of the slippage is not that, instead of a statue, you will be putting a (soon conventional) mobile in place, but a slippery slope.

There may be, then, as in the Serial Threshold Theory of cell *regeneration* (e.g., if a worm is cut in two, why does one part grow a head and the other a tail?), some limit to the process of recurrence where (as is already happening in performance) a distinct message is transmitted through the noise, an (undeniable?) act of communication (aesthetically unorthodox but a matter of survival) in that ecliptic moment before reversal begins (as in the instant of the worm's severance)—as if deciphering in the redundancy, through the signifying chains of the DNA, the originary code of the Eternal Return.

Which brings us back to the prison-house of language where, in the profusions of desire, there is still the desire for meaning. In the sixties, the kinesthetic intensity of the most innovative theatre, largely without words, *looked* like dance, where words, if they occurred at all, were objects or impulsions or random expletives of air, as they still are in the spectacles of Wilson. Across the gulf of language, one of the important rediscoveries of the period was the inseparability of actor and dancer in the theatre forms of the Far East, which are entering the structure of innovation, even while some are trying to renovate the classics, not through daring new conceptions, but by redressing them as Kabuki, Topeng, Jatra, or Saraikella Chhau.

If recent theatre was chastened by this conspicuous memory of a common source with dance, bringing words back to the body, there is still in the theatre that other reflex, from the engrailed memory of our dramatic literature, that wants to bring the body back alive to the words, words, words, and wants them, moreover, to amount to something, for "Nothing will come of nothing," as we see in *Lear*. That, too, as we learned from Beckett, can be *done*; and the wonder of it was an immense reversal of theatrical entropy from the holding action of the Cold War into the synergies of the sixties. The release took place at the last articulate margins of thought where, in our avant-garde tradition, we have come to expect the real energy of innovation to come forth. That is not, however, at all the case in the German theatre today, which was early on hospitable to Beckett and has a long investment in the classical drama of words.

Despite its equally long investment in bureaucracy and the industrialization of theatre skills, the huge governmentally-sponsored apparatus in Germany is apparently more active with innovation than small groups trying to survive outside the system. In a collaborative form, there's an experimental advantage in established continuity. There's also the anxiety that liberation by subsidy makes for the kind of experiment that is technocratic, replaying the bourgeois Text on the electronic turntables and computerized switchboards. Theatre activity started up in the ruins of World War II even before public transportation and the newspapers, but what Brecht said at his first rehearsal in East Berlin seems to linger on as a recurring suspicion: "The stage [East and West] gives off a strange aura of harmlessness . . . as if Hitler had also used up the meanness of the Germans. . . ." I don't pretend to be an authority on the degree of meanness revived in the German theatre of the last decade, but I was in Frankfurt last year on the night when the radical theatre TAT did its farewell performance, right after the general election, when the CDU came in and closed it. At the time we

were told by our German friends that only the classics could carry the
burden of experiment anymore because, through long familiarity, they
were considered harmless, however renovated.

Nevertheless, I also saw in Frankfurt—on the black box of a nearly
empty space, with a scrimmed fluorescent cube suspended menacingly
above, like a block of Euclidéan thought or the reflexive
negative/positive of the white geometry of the corporate structure
across the street (it might have been a bank), in turn reflecting in plate
glass and plastic skin the Mies-en-same of the theatre building itself—a
version of the Sophocles/Hölderlin *Antigone*, which included a long-
haired Creon in black jeans who evolved (like student leaders of the sixties) into a business suit, and a punk-rock chorus from an S/M cabaret,
who humiliated Antigone to death. Over a lowered trestle on the
forestage, like a customs barrier (*"I can't go to Europe without a
passport!"* American actors screamed in the sixties, though they went to
Europe), an incriminating arc of white light splayed over the audience,
who argued loudly in the lobby afterward, both the charges of collusion and the issue of political censorship. Again, equivocal feelings.
The staging was presented as an alternative to the one-dimensional
thinking about a politics otherwise controlled by the media, which
hardly allows a single coherent thought. Who could doubt that it was
an intelligent and valuable performance? Who could doubt that the
media-controlled politics was going about its business as usual?

If I've been backing away to the sixties for perspective on what's
happening now, the reasons are all palpable in that offbeat production
on an affluent stage in Germany, where the repercussions of that
period are still being played out, as they are in Squat, organized as a
commune in still-affluent America, and living from hand to mouth. As
compared to Squat, the young director of *Antigone*, Christof Nel, was
in a compromised situation, with all those technological resources con-
tradicting his politics, though he tried to minimize the resources to
avoid it. As with Ariane Mnouchkine at the Théâtre du Soleil, some
German directors shift the resources to other sites, like factories or
movie houses. But there is also in certain German directors—as with
the French usurper Patrice Chéreau at Bayreuth—the desire to use
resources extravagantly to compromise the situation, like the Pop Art
grotesqueries of *Buhnenraum* (the new scene design) or the production
of *The Winter's Tale* with Mattel (the toymaker's) slime all over the
stage. Sometimes there is merely an extravagant compromise and, in
the prosperous atmosphere of the state theatres, a feeling of the right
political opinions in an indifferent place; or a kind of token politics
uneasily remembering its dissident roots; or a kind of affectation of
poverty. Sometimes, still, there is no affectation, only extravagance.

Chéreau's postindustrial version of *The Ring of the Nibelungen*

(1976), with Pierre Boulez as musical director, was another matter: the right place, a shrine, chosen for the extravagance. Chéreau saw in the divided Wotan an abyss between the music and the drama, in which the music disavows the ideology of Wagner's text. It seems an easy way of letting Wagner off the hook, though quite consistent with the program of deconstruction, undoing the threads of the illusory fabric, letting the components have their say not in concert but in contestation with each other. The anecdotal score—overpowered by its own insurgency—culminates in a concluded music and an indeterminate drama, which causes Boulez to feel a cyclical impulse where everything begins again, with a Wotan 2 and a Wotan 3, in a sort of Fibonnaci spiral that might have been scored at the electronic music studio at Beaubourg. At Bayreuth, where the Text is nearly Sacred, the supernal Wagnerian Myth was shown to be biodegradable, recycled as bourgeois melodrama. There was an uproar. But elsewhere, the spectres of Myth and Archetype also linger in contemporary performance, as at the Jungian doors of perception.

If the sixties were a time when the technocracy was rabidly assaulted, they were also a time when, against the power of the technocracy, the technological was also occulted. Marshall McLuhan was the shamanic voice. In "the mosaic world of implosion," we were told, video invokes "archaic tribal ghosts of the most vigorous brand." It was in an American tradition of cranky prophecy. "See, they return," wrote Ezra Pound years before, but not for the sixties the "tentative/ Movements" and "slow feet"—rather the polymorphous clamor of Love's Body, and high decibels; from which the Chorus of the Frankfurt *Antigone* was derived, like the murderous Altamont Festival from the Love-In at Woodstock. In the Age of Aquarius, there were contradictions in the acoustics as in the communes, and a dream of Eden in computer feedback. Embracing stimulus with stumuli, we would conduct "transactions" with the means of regimentation. Or, taking vows of poverty, plunge into the accelerating dance of Shiva. Whether with oscillators, amplifiers and light projections or chanting pyramids of doctrinaire flesh, as in The Living Theater's *Frankenstein*, the senses were assaulted until illusion took over, disabling the boundaries of art and life.

The boundaries still stand, of course, as stubbornly as the Berlin Wall. There were, in the sixties, other more beguiling versions of that disabling tendency, in the tradition of Duchamp and Cage. The landmass relocations (over the transcontinental telephone) and moveable feasts of the Fluxus group, who performed everything from the making of salads to mixed-media variations on the Cageian Silence, were also epistemological conundrums. Ubiquitous, domestic and cosmic, an overflow of the fifties, they were the jetset of World-Play. If not apocalyptic, they were still inconoclastic; and in the performances of Dick Higgins or Nam June Paik could also be manically aggressive, as when Higgins speeded through a crowd with a (poisonous?) uroboric snake in the air, or Nam June smashed up pianos. The afterimages of Fluxus are still influential, though there was also something effete about it—too aesthetically riddling—for the raw political fervor of the sixties, with its "self-help" auxiliary of crash therapies, mass arrests, decision-making processes, Encounter groups, and karate. These tendencies have in turn influenced the new performance Activities of charter members of Fluxus, such as George Brecht and Allan Kaprow, who did the first memorable Happening and a transitional event in which a Wall made of iceblocks was constructed and melted, proving that art can do what the world can't.

In the eighties, whatever's left of the Movement has grown tentative again as, at the level of World-Play, inflation dances grotesquely with recession and politics drags its feet. And none of this might mean much to our theme if the spinoff hadn't found its dizzy way, like the aftermath of Sufi whirling—the long diminuendo of which we see in Wilson's operas—into advanced performance theory, experimental practice, and conventional theatre, as into the circling stylistics of postmodern thought, which thinks of itself, vertiginously, *as* performance, "a whole carnal stereophony," as Roland Barthes embraces it in *The Pleasure of the Text*.

Eroticizing the Text is to make of it a graph of intensities arising from a libidinal source moving over a surface that has no interior, a labyrinth of excitations without signals. If an intensity has a shape, it has no future. It is not a project. Intensities are unnameable because anonymous. In this view, the theatre is a space of intensities with no other presence but itself, atemporal, neither the movement of an a priori nor the incursion of nothingness upon the inaugural moment, only the intrinsic contours of the libidinal flow, with its glandular displacements in the acting body. But if the intensity is anonymous, it is also—for reasons beyond knowing—*amortized*, and it is the space of amortization which is the theatre that *remembers*, staking out identities and slowing down the intensities. It's these slowed-down intensities that Jean-François Lyotard perceives in artists today who are, like Daniel Buren, engaged "not in the destruction of significations but in extending the limits of sense perception: making visible (or audible) what now goes unobserved, through the alteration of sense data, perception itself." That's undeniably so, and a modest proposition for art as compared to the short time ago when the analogy between "language-games" and "art-games"—asserted by Lyotard *as* analogy, but still assuming the *games*—was suspended with other distinctions, as if in the pure hegemony of play there could be the path of an excitation without memory.

So it was thought, or desired, in the sixties. And if not, why not? In the theatricalizing of everyday life, the choice seemed to be for those with half a heart: *play, or be played upon.* In the politicizing of theatrical life, there seemed to be no choice—as in the antioedipal seizure of the Odéon in 1968, and the pathos of Jean-Louis Barrault, who tried to mediate things with the students and ended up being fired by Malraux. You all remember the specific intensities, the spectacles and farcical *lazzi* of the time, from the levitation of the Pentagon by the Yippies to the mortification of Che Guevara by the Bolivian generals. The repertoire was catalogued in a rather exultant issue on "Politics and Performance," in the summer of 1969 by *The Drama Review*, then the leading theatre journal in America. Judging the photographed exposure of the dead Che as a repressive spectacle that failed, the overview was that "we seem to have entered an era in which the human dramatic potential is to be realized foremostly in life and for life. The stage once again follows along."

But follows to what end? Life, as the theatre well knows, mystifies the demystifiers. An irony of our reflective distancing from the period is that what appeared to be superficial or became faddish also acquired ideological force. Take one apparent fad, virtually named in the passage quoted: the Human Potential Movement. As it developed and diversified, from Esalen and EST to Deleuze and Guattari—even appropriating Grotowski, paratheatrically, on behalf of life—the drama dropped out of "the human dramatic potential" along with the oedipal narrative, and the human seemed to be following after, dropped by theory, a mere fissure in the anonymous order of things, the ultimate bourgeois illusion, concussively figured in the duplicities of language, with its seemingly impermeable calculus of representations. Which is how we came, in theory, to what is desirably left: the intensities of the *pure potential*. There was an intimation of this dispossessed energy of disjunctions in the jubilatory discourse—the "divine apathia divine athambia divine aphasia"—of the prophetically berserk Lucky in *Waiting for Godot*. That demented plainsong of love's bereft body, rejecting figuration, is also the topological model for the unmediated presence of the aphasic (Christopher Knowles) in Robert Wilson's *The Life and Times of Joseph Stalin*, and the subsequent conversion of various types of dysfunction into a communal energy in Wilson's theatre compositions, with their stunning deployment of outer space as a Moebius strip of *in*-determinable life—which is not the surface of a depth.

What has been sought for in experiment under the name of Artaud is a new volumetrics of theatre, in the space of the spectator who is permeated by what, then, is admissible as representation. In this seizure of a space (within), the volume unfolded cannot be reduced by speech, nor reduced *to* speech. It is a *spacing* produced by the incitation of a time which disobeys the Word and its patrimony of phonic linearity, like aphasia, a resonance of the subject in the space of words between culture and the inner ear, a voice without rhetoric.

The end or closure of representation is, in this vision, "original representation," according to Derrida on Artaud, "autorepresentation of pure visibility and even pure sensibility." Wilson's imagination appears to close upon this state. The aphasic, with the virtue of pure sensibility, has not only been given a consecrated space in the performance, but the performance gathers itself around him as a structurating force. That there is therapy in the process is a purely coincidental by-product of the aesthesis, and the therapy is mutual. What has been done is to bring into performance for the sake of performance something like the post-Laingian dispensation of Deleuze and Guattari, a strain of thought still drawing on the radicalized "politics of experience" and the ethos of disjunction. Beckett's mouth, Artaud's body without organs, and the breasts of Tiresias on the naked torso of the hallucinating Judge Schreber act together—like images out of Wilson, Squat, Zadek, Ronconi, or Terayama—to describe an autoerotic delirium that is, in the words of the *Anti-Oedipus*, "an intense feeling of transition, states of pure naked intensity stripped of all shape or form. . . . Nothing here is representative; rather it is all life and lived experience: . . ."

We keep circling back to the intensities because, despite the slowing down, they are still being sought for. Another approach to the pure naked experience—more specifically atavistic—is the recent quest of Jerzy Grotowski for a "Theater of Sources." In the celebratory paratheatrics of *Holiday* and *The Tree of People*, Grotowski seems to be after a more elitist version of the participatory utopianism of the sixties, by which he was stricken when he first came to the United States. Is it theatre? What he is doing sounds, through the rash of skeptical and rapturous reports—torchlight processions in the forest, honey-dipping meditations, and the laying on of hands, like a Gothic renascence of Gestalt therapy. But Grotowski has been, and may still be (though I distrust the messianism) one of the more seminal artists of our time; and the theory for what he is doing may be found in Derrida's essay on Artaud, to whom Grotowski was originally indebted, in the hermetic formalism of his early work.

In the essay (in *Writing and Difference*), Derrida speaks of the higher politics of the Festival, a return through the initiatory trace to the abrogation of all binaries, and the disappearance of theatre into itself. Since the spectator is impregnated with the spectacle he cannot project it scopically, which is a way of warding off the reality of those powers which, threatening in life, are celebrated in the Festival, which "must be a political *act*. And the *act* of political revolution is *theatrical*." It is important to realize, in the de-definitions of art, that not all circles are the same circle, as this revolutionary circle back to theatre is not quite the circle of *The Eighteenth Brumaire*, from tragedy to farce (which requires parallax rather than impregnation), because it is a conception projected outside of history, where the theatre exists only in a perpetual present. In that scene, what appears to be repetition is not, and that's what we want destroyed. For the Enemy *is* repetition, the life-denying force of a cadaverous return, where the present holds on for dear life, coming into Being, the Enemy of the libidinal body, negativity incarnate, ungenerous, since it refuses the present to death, wanting to preserve its illusion. The Festival would consume it at once, leaving nothing to be repeated, *not a trace*—"expenditure without economy, without reserve, without return, without history." The power of theatre is an *abandonment*—both the wildness and the discard—a politics with neither property nor propriety, where "the origin," already *within* representation, "is always *penetrated*."

We can only anticipate the time with what Henry James, a stylist almost as labyrinthine as Derrida—abandoned *by* the theatre to the specular intricacies of the Novel—called somewhere "a reflective gape." Meanwhile, *in* the theatre that we know, in the immediacy of its wildest new forms, there is the pressure of old compulsion. Whether consciousness pretends to cosmic proportions or contracts to a needle's eye, it must certainly see the pretense in the performance.

Where's the action? they were asking, as everybody was making a scene, or putting a body on the line. When we looked around, however, to check the line, it seemed to have disappeared, going through a series of indeterminable behaviors from action to activism to atavism, while the overdeterminations of emergent French Freud gave theoretical grounding to the idea of disappearance as the subject of performance, the self-consuming thing itself.

It may have been something of a coda to the period which haunts us like those archaic tribal ghosts, when a young man with self-cancelling propensities, who had previously had himself crucified on a Volkswagen, took up the proposition of disappearance as a cue for performance and, after duly publicizing his intention, literally vanished. His real name is appropriately Chris Burden, and I believe it was for three days. It was not entirely clear when he returned *the degree to which* that was the Same—the anamnesic horror of the repetitive play of disappearance, like the follicles of the Freudian *Fort/Da*, not play but the *remission* of play—the critical problem of performance, along with the problem of *Who cares?* For if the Enemy is repetition, the repetition is *in* the play, both a limit and a spur (Derrida's *éperon*) to innovation, to which performance wants at *its* limit to put a stop. We see that, literally, in Alan Sonfist's conception of a *rigor mortis* whereby he would deed his dead body to a museum. When I say, Who cares? I mean that in the declensions of performance from the public scene and the magnitudes of political action to the autisms of Body Art and the new modes of confessional performance, we are once again reconceiving, as with the aphasic, the idea of an audience, its prerogatives, propriety and scale, and the old question of wisdom in numbers. Sonfist's performance of his last will and testament, his naked body on a glass-enclosed slab, is the absolute inversion—in the body Artaud detested—of the naked streaming sonorous realization he discerned in Plato's allusions to the Orphic Mysteries.

If there is anything to be concluded from this dispensation of ceaseless beginnings, it is that there is something lethal in a pure physiology of performance—a desideratum of material murmurs that speak of forgetfulness and death. In the imagination of Artaud it comes with equivocal reverence for the holiness of the acting body. The metaphysics through the skin would just as well, in a ceaseless sparagmos, tear the body apart; or there is a kind of fierce tumerous gloating over the progressive accompaniment of death, as over the bubos of the Plague, as if the time of theatre were a kind of Veronica-dance over the already-bled eyeballs of that *other* time, which we'll never forget.

Trying to forget is perhaps the most painful theoretical problem with which we are still wrestling in performance. The sixties took up, as if it were canonical, the "active forgetfulness" of Nietzsche and tried to enact it into being until, in the intensities of the Resistance, it felt legislated. The agency of the desire-to-forget was the self-estranging subject of the play-within-the-play, denying where it came from and starting all over again, until the action we were looking for, just as it came into focus, seemed to pass out of sight. The disappearance of what we sought for is the function of a longing for an unimpoverished plural, the full benison of a life pushing beyond representation, a Text which, like a field of gazing grain, extends *"as far as the eye can reach"* (Barthes). But the reach is also deadly, and we can't forget that, as the theatre never does, desiring *less* theatre in its crucial difference from life.

In the eighties, the outward appearances are less apocalyptic, but we are by no means free of the suffusion of life with theatre. We can see it in politics, fashion, poetics, therapy, reception theory, ethnography, and advanced critical discourse, where the terminology of performance is so prevalent we are likely to think of innovation as *nothing but* performance, taking *absolutely for granted* that you can't tell, for instance, the dancer from the dance—which was always an open question. As for the politics of performance and the performance of politics—and the shift in authoritarian modes—we see in the prolonged negotiations for the hostages in Iran a spectacular demonstration (*and* remonstrance) of that structural indeterminacy that was the participatory ideal of the sixties and the deconstructionist ideal of the seventies, a paradigm of uncentering authority, heterotopic, polyvalent, and tapelooped for speculation, where in the field of the subject there is no referent, like an avant-garde text described by Barthes, whose specific nature is *uncertain*, and which can neither be classified nor judged nor—in *Le chantage à la theorie*—its immediate or eventual future predicted. "Yet this quality," as Barthes understood, "is a blackmail *as well* (theory blackmailed): love me, keep me, defend me, since I conform to the theory you call for; do I not do what Artaud, Cage, etc., have done?—But Artaud is not just 'avant-garde'; he is a kind of writing *as well*; Cage has a certain charm *as well* . . . —But those are *precisely* the attributes which are not recognized by theory, which are sometimes execrated by theory. At least make your taste and your ideas match, etc. (*The scene continues, endlessly.*)"

And so it does in Iran, asking our aesthetics to put up or shut up in political terms, matching taste to ideas as we helplessly observe the ceaseless deferrals in practice, outwardly masculine, but labile, feminine, veiled, a metonymic miracle of shifting power—from the militants in the embassy to President Bani-Sadr to Foreign Minister Ghotzbzadeh to the Revolutionary Council to the Ayatollah Khomeini, who purportedly has the last word about which we can't entirely be sure, like a sybilline echo of the instituted trace. In this situational ethic where no answer is prefigured, we have a suggestion perhaps that structures which are alluring and supportable in art may be simply intolerable in life, depending on what game you're playing on which side of the demon of analogy, and whether or not you are the hostage, as you are to theory, where we are at a semiological loss to make distinctions about the indeterminacy. It may seem insufficiently theoretical, but it is also tempting to think—at this turn of the Viconian gyre of performance—that our next major innovations are likely to come from those who absolutely *refuse* to play games, upping the ante on illusion, and thereby improving the quality of the play. The risk is clear in politics which is, so long as you *see* the illusion, an object lesson to art.

Look What Thy Memory
Cannot Contain

●

THE MORE VALIANT EFFORTS TO THEATRICALIZE EXPERIENCE—TO
make plays which are not scripted enactments in a predetermined space
but the act itself in the living *now*—ended abruptly with the Vietnam
War. There was, recently, a sort of sad memory trace, a tamed enactment, in the disguised surfacing of Abbie Hoffman. Timed as it was to
the publishing of his new book, there was an afterimage of enterprising
dissidence, ripping off the media in a new bourgeois role, but not urg-
ing us to play ours with the old instant gratifications. While the attempt to politicize theatre along with the theatricalizing of politics
didn't prevail (there are still insurrectionary pockets in the theatre,
with politics little but image), some are discomfited that it didn't. We
miss the volatile energy in the radical critique of theatrical value. Actually, we have no radical critique, never did. What seemed like it in
the late sixties was haphazard, without theory or continuity. It came
and went. When the most spectacular activism went underground,
there were rumors it was developing theory. Logically so. The
underground is the natural habitat and congenital analogue of theory.
Or so we might gather from literary theory, immersed in the processes
of the unconscious, where the activism of the sixties seems to have been
sublimated, with an upped ante of unnegotiable *desire*, the theory
behaving like theatre, almost making the theatre superfluous.

Not only in literature but in other disciplines we see the dominion of
the performance principle. But as they talk about performance in, say,
the act of reading, few of those who talk about it really care at all
about the theatre, or know very much about it. Our men of letters,
unlike those of Europe, do not take to the theatre naturally, and our
women of letters take more naturally to film. The image-marketing of

the woman's body in the reproductive apparatus makes it the inevitable staging-place of feminist theory. The theatre is also subject to reproduction, but as it has never been very literary in this country, it has never been very theoretical either. In all the experimental activity of the last generation, there was no systematic effort to lay bare, as a political act, the processes of representation; nor has there been anything like a conscious, no less collective, articulation of theatrical ideology, as there was in France and Germany after the uprising of 1968.

We needn't claim any miracles there to sense a significant difference from what didn't happen here. Our theatre tradition, such as it is, remains anti-intellectual, like our political tradition. While there has been some shifting around of performance to other environments, and some loose theory about that, it is nothing like the intricately scanned displacements of the "privileged space" of performance which have been studied elsewhere as a manifestation of the linguistic shifter, with its ideological repercussions in the unconscious. It was an ideological cleansing of the unconscious that was demanded by the protocols of Avignon in July 1968 (after the banning of The Living Theater), which refused "the distinction between artistic activities and political, social, or everyday ones."

For a while, in the streets and in the factories, the emphasis was on the demystified surface of things. When the unconscious returned to performance, it was—by an infusion of French Freud and revisionist Marx—weighted with politics, relocated in history. In Stuttgart or Bochum, we may now see revisionist Shakespeare in a kind of Lacanian aftermath of the Frankfurt School. The theory knows the liabilities. Since the most experimental work in Germany is being done not underground, but within the affluent framework of the state-subsidized theatres, the young socialist directors worry about preëmptive tolerance. Yet the work has scale and theoretical dimension, and there is nothing comparable in the apolitical and untheorized mediocrity of our own Regional Theatres. In what is called Alternative Theatre, the scattered remnants of a politics are rather feeble. There is nothing even vaguely at the same level of political consciousness. What is really disturbing is to think we have come away from the period (now being reassessed) with no better grasp of history, nor the theatre's place in it, than we had when, in order to avoid the preëmption, we tried to do without history almost entirely.

There is a sense in which we thought, in the more experimental work of recent years, to restore theatre to time by ignoring time, or overdoing it, as in the aphasic and cataleptic spectacles of Robert Wilson. In the reflux of theatre through Performance Art (the theatricalizing of the gallery-system), there is the immanence of *a continuous present*, and the ongoing allure of indeterminacy. "I'm not a historian," said Gogo, waiting at the end of the fifties, unable to remember one moment from another, giving the cue (through a misprision of Beckett's desperate forgetting) for a lapse of memory. As we improvised upon the moment, we thought we were liberated from history, which plays upon our vanities in turn.

In life, in theatre, in theory, we forget how thoroughly improvisation is coded, the libidinal body an agglomerate of old reflexes which are, in the discipline of an actor's repetitive craft, rehearsed away from banality before the breakthrough. In other disciplines, we look to performance as a mode of purer freedom, while our ideas of performance (usually retrograde) come from an institution which is historically overdetermined. As the theatre itself borrows from behavioral and structural theories borrowed from the theatre—like Barthes' performative pleasures of the text or Goffman's dramatistic *Presentation of the Self in Everyday Life*—we find ourselves tautologically recycled into a double bind, with a solipsistic flash of history in the momentary brilliance, like the long bright steel safety pin, invoking Achaean spears, in Molly Bloom's stained and scented drawers. The recursive attenuations of Wilson's operas or other serial performances (or soap operas for that matter) may—like Molly's monologue—go on forever, but only within the theatre of language, as along the walls of a conceptual prison, which is, even with diminished verbalization, still reflected in the language of theatre.

Which is to say: as other disciplines try to open themselves to a prospective field of infinite play, with the theatre as a structural model, we can only see the possibilities of a newer theatre from perspectives inscribed upon us by the old, with its inevitable circumscription of play. As we deconstruct the stage or change environments or play in the round, the sightlines are probably ineradicable because indelibly in the mind. Perspective is troubling. We thought we could expose the ideological recessions, the hidden motives of time, by developing techniques of alienation, as in Brecht, or strategies of ontological disruption, as in Foreman, to take things out of the falsifying appearance of perspective, and tip them up front. We'd back off to see better or simply take things apart, to see how they really work. But when we looked another time, every exposure was a secretion. The form is ghosted, as we are, by the mental habits of the form, which encrust our habits of perception. The very words we use to talk about perception we have acquired from the theatre, where the ghosting, as on the ramparts, recedes into its language, unable to unfold the tale because of the secret interdiction of its prison-house. When we think of the powers of representation, we feel them irreparably connected to that—the power behind the image that *is* exposed, and there is the paranoia that comes from the realization that it can never be anything but an image, as time goes out of mind.

If we are to continue, however, in the *making* of history—that is, exercising through the theatre some measure of control of our presence in it—our work must include a critique of the illusion of an uninterrupted present, keeping it in mind. It is an illusion that has its analogue in the Energy Crisis, which came not only from heedlessness of the future but from thinking of the future as having no reality but the moment. For the moment that may be so, but there are moments and moments and, like a birthing over the grave, the *matter* of duration. Artaud's proclamation of no more masterpieces and his alchemical passion for a theatre of dematerializing presence was the apocalyptic expression of a critical ambivalence: at this moment, the desire to get outside historical time and its petrifying infection of culture; at the same time, a longing for the seeds, origins, traces, the lost shadows (or Double) of time. Thus, the nostalgia for the archaic and, without Artaud's self-punishing asepsis, the recent sentimentalization of ritual. In the metalanguage of theatre envisaged by Artaud—a mnemotechnic physiology of diaphanous signs—we see the lineaments of an infinite regression, a mortifying self-consciousness at those filamenting nerve-ends of thought which, because it has no grounds for a theory of self-consciousness, is ultimately victimized by history.

Having experienced an era of theatricality in public life, our current dilemma—in the wary quiescence of the eighties—is whether we are strategically capable in the theatre of conceiving the work-in-progress with respect to a determinate historical situation, what is really in the here-and-now, not disincluding the myth of a perpetual present. As we survey, however, the recent past, it seems important to remember—in terms by which theatre *is* indissolubly merged with life: time, the body, passing—what it is that we *have* experienced; in short, that there was a past, and that it insists upon being present. Just as we now sense a sort of collective amnesia, right and left, over the late-lamented atrocities of the Vietnam War (and a collective inability to know what we should think about it if it weren't forgotten), there is a tendency in the theatre to forget what delusions of theatre had been sponsored by quite intelligent people in our time *because* they were opposed to the Vietnam War.

For instance: there was, in the mid-sixties, an issue of our major theatre journal—more polemical then, insistently "objective" now—on "Politics and Performance," with a section documenting a series of events which in their theatricality seemed to demonstrate both the uselessness of conventional theatre and the transfer to the political realm of the (illusory) power of theatre to activate human affairs: "We seem to have entered an era in which the human dramatic potential is to be realized foremostly in life, and for life. The stage once again follows along." It is following more slowly today, as performance bleeds into theory, but it is chastening to study the accounts of the occupation of the library at Columbia, a Paris barricade in the Days of May, the Pentagon besieged, and the mortification of Che Guevera, described as a perversion of theatre through which shines, in the exposed dead body, the pure exemplary act. Elsewhere, there were articles on the happenings of the Dutch PROVOS and other forms of street and guerrilla theatre, as well as an article on "Booking the Revolution." I admire still the grit and fury of it all, but there was practically no cogent thought about it in the issue, nor about what was then called (by liberal sympathizers) Third Theater, and we have come to realize that it came to no more profound an end than the mission of Che in Bolivia or, somewhat later, the massacre of the pathetic renegades of the SLA by the assembled might of the Los Angeles police force. Since that time, while we have had to think hard about a possible politics, not sure that it is, there has been very little said, in the theatre, in this country, about politics and performance.

The extermination of the self-dramatizing comrades of Patty Hearst as if they were Vietcong in the jungle was a fittingly ironic coda to all the previously theatricalized dissent. (Or maybe the better coda was the mysterious recidivism of Tanya/Patty, painting her fingernails and reading fashion magazines and sneaking out with her family and an array of bodyguards for dinner at Fisherman's Wharf, to which her resentencing seemed an anti-climax, like her subsequent marriage to one of the bodyguards.) Because there were other illusions of perception involved in this aberration of history, I'd like to say a little more about it. The pitiable carnage was also a television spectacular, on prime time, and was completed like any good TV script (for which it might have been confused if you tuned in late) in just about an hour of performance. The media had been served as it had been served by other famous performance events on which recent docudramas have been modeled (on the network principle that you can't have too much of a good thing): the killing of Lee Harvey Oswald, the terrorism at the Munich Olympics, the assasination of Bobby Kennedy.

It is a commonplace by now that the point of view in front of a TV set blurs the distinction between the real and the invented or, as with *Holocaust*, the unspeakability of the subject and the solicitations of empathy, to say nothing of its being presented between the solicitations of unspeakable commercials. There was always a certain radical exultancy in pointing out that the auto-da-fé in the Los Angeles ghetto might have been staged in a studio or on location, like the simulations of moon landings. But as we ask, who would have known the difference? we fall prey to imitative form. For, we were also presented with scenarios of radical activism as if the dramaturgical difference between life and theatre was inconsequential, or the blurring of the difference desirable. While the activism seems over with, there are still those, in art and theory, excited by the duplicities, caught up in the mirroring game. That is not, however, the deepest game of theatre, whose ontological nature *is* duplicitous—which is why the most powerful tradition of theatre is to resist its own powers, distrusting its appearances and critically testing its capacity for self-deception, sometimes by reducing the theatre in theatre and sometimes by increasing it, keeping everything in us alive to *the idea of difference*, lest we be too easily absorbed into the stream of fantasy.

The perception of difference is the groundroot of criticism—of which, in the proliferation of performance events, we have had very little that is valuable. Among those interested in experimental tendencies, there has been little serious assessment of what has been seen and said and what it purports to *mean*, through the orthodoxy of non-meanings, if anything at all. There has been small discourse, mainly description of whatever happens to come along and temporarily fill the scene. It's as if, after the indiscriminate partisanship of the sixties, there's a freeze on the passion for distinction. The performance activity is presented in documentary fashion, on the assumption that it will speak for itself if merely described. Of course it will do nothing of the kind. It will only speak for the descriptions, which make everything, the real achievements and the junk, feel qualitatively alike—and all somewhat lifeless. Elsewhere, too, it's as if the work had nothing substantial to say and wasn't meant to be taken seriously as constructs of meaning. At the most sophisticated levels of interpretation, as in structuralist thought, the issue of quality is rarely dealt with. There would appear to be no grounds for it. That's a meaning that needs some critical thought. As for the kind of popular criticism we are beginning to hear about the excesses of theatre directors in revisionist productions (from some who originally encouraged tendencies they should have been critical of to begin with), it seems to me misguided and boorish. I am referring to those who, after being disappointed by the crudities of Serban's *The Cherry Orchard* or Schechner's *Oedipus*, are now warning us off overtamperings with the classics and the directorial arrogance which is presumably taking over the theatre by demeaning the playwright.

We are advised, by Richard Gilman, for instance, that "classic texts exist and have their rights." So they do, and they will no doubt survive the most arrogant of us. That being so, there's no reason in the world why Serban or Schechner shouldn't continue to rethink the classics in accordance with not only their own needs as theatre artists but the new vectors of history by which the classics are crossed. It would be valuable, however, if what is being rethought could enter some in-

telligible continuity (if not community) of discourse. I would like to
hear more about the motives behind the worst excesses and most heavy-
handed overlays or the most subversive interpretations. When they
were being praised, one heard very little about the validity of the *ideas*
in the work of Serban or Schechner or, as far back as *Marat/Sade*, the
more celebrated work of Peter Brook. I have seen, so far as I can
remember, no rigorous analysis of the conspicuous illusions in Brook's
theories of language and sound (taken over by Serban), nor of
Schechner's Environmental Theater, especially in relation to his own
practice. (On older and rather proprietary, but very respectable,
academic grounds, there was such a critique some years ago, of Brook's
King Lear, and mine, in a book by the Shakespearean scholar Maynard
Mack. I doubt that it was seen by many people in the theatre or those
worrying about revisionism now, who would have scorned it then,
when they were encouraging the improvisational banalities of the
Open Theater or the paradistic crudities of *Macbird!*) Instead of being
told to cease and desist, directors should be critically encouraged—challenged if necessary—to think better, harder, farther,
whether in or through or around or without classical texts, whether
respecting the perceived purity of an interior design or fracturing it for
other historical or aesthetic purposes.

As for the rights of the texts, in an era of "intertextuality" those
rights are at least questionable. Some of the best minds of our age, bor-
rowing much from the concept of performance, have been strenuously
and imaginatively denying not only the privileged authority in politics
but the authorial principle in literature, developing theories of
metatexts and paracriticism, and there's surely good motive for the
theatre to be reflecting that out of natural instincts of its own. It would
be remiss and retrograde if it didn't—though for the most part, true,
that's not exactly what's been happening, not with the same conceptual
rigor, in the deconstructed versions of the classics. But the necessity of
the deconstructions was foreseen through the history of modernist
drama, from the avalanches of Ibsen through the lost records and missing author of Pirandello to the tapeloops of Beckett and the disjunct
fantasies in the mirrored brothel of Genet, which ends with the exposure of the audience in the replicative falsity of theatre, in the in-
terstitial moment crossing art and life, where all the dualisms begin
again.

At its best, the desire of art, and thought, given over to performance
is to collapse the painful dualities with which philosophy has struggled
since its inception, the dualities tangled in the language by which they
are named: mind/body, self/substance, spirit/matter, surface/depth,
truth/illusion, I/Other, word/thing, being/becoming, letting be;
always, however, keeping a cliff-hanging finger on the critical dif-

ference. The potency of performance may, as distinctions blur, almost be measured by the acuity of that perilous act. It is an act all the more difficult to perform as the divisions are doubled over in the Lacanian mirror, with its stagings of identity. The impoverishment of performance may, as the plot becomes a process, almost be measured by resistance to the process, as the actor plays the same old role in a repertoire of familiar gestures, or slightly updated facsimiles. In my own work, with the KRAKEN group, there was always an impulse toward collapsing dualities, or the image of such a collapse carried away by the reflexive process, and flooded with interpretations—as a reaction against the seemingly exhausted dramatizations of the divided self. This went, however, against the grain of my own nature, which was bored by easy indeterminacies, distrusted the aleatory, and sought closure. We were sorely troubled, then, by the decentrifugal force of the work throwing off meaning(s) at each stage—say, the atomization of character into the dynamics of the ensemble, the structural web of indeterminate relations, which seemed like a gesture toward wholeness by the denial of wholeness.

It is a contradiction that we can't even vaguely pretend to have resolved, though it made energies available to performance that would otherwise have been arrested. (Despite my own reservations about the dispersions and textual plenitudes of structuralist process, the same may be said of critical theory: unless the decentering impulse is felt, explored, allowed to take its course—not merely dismissed as fashion—we will not have avoided turning criticism into exhibitionism but, rather, will have subsided prematurely into *conventional* performance, where the poverty of interpretation is safer in thought, and very little distinction *has* to be made.) Nor—as we scattered character into semblances, shadows, doubles, projections and intimations, the merest resonance of an allusion to an identity—was it a matter of carrying the de-realization of behavior to its limit as a mere formal proposition. The experiment was, rather, a struggle through our sense of splitting behaviors—spellbound by the mirror we wanted to destroy—into something like an affirmation of the Reality Principle.

If the fractured tale were told, the illusion of wholeness seemed as destructive of human capability as the absence of wholeness. Yet it is the desire to achieve wholeness, to reduce the immanence of absence (or its propaganda), that accounts for the drift of performance back toward life, when it occurs. Our work was highly charged in the body, ideographic, but everytime we came back, we ran into language, and the ubiquitous tangle of words—whether we worked with a classic text, or without it.

The sticking point of theatre during the last generation—relating the politics of performance to aboriginal states and ritual forms, over a grid of illusion—was language: what to do with it, what to make of it, how to disemburden the playing space of it, and whether, at any level of being, we can do without it. The more drastic experiments with the discard or disintegration of language are just about over, the ritual frenzy has departed, and there is something of a revival of interest in words. Since it's not at all conclusive that the words of the tribe have been purified, it's important to remember what was done, why, and to determine where it leaves us. There are all kinds of illusions, but perhaps the best we can do, as Eliot once said, is to improve their quality—and there are still those fostered by doing the right thing for the wrong reasons, or the wrong thing for the right reasons. After a while, we yield up our sense of right and wrong, throwing distinction to the winds, not because we have grown any more generous in our capacities, only perceptually less scrupulous.

A while ago, for instance, there was a new piece performed in New York and at the New Theater Festival in Baltimore (where I saw it) by a Japanese company trained in Kendo and directed by Yoshi, who has worked in the vocal experiments of Brook and Serban. A note in the program says that the language of the piece would be inaccessible even to a Japanese audience, since it stands in relation to current speech as Latin to modern English. Therefore, the work—which is highly orchestrated and strongly performed—can be perceived mainly at a tactile and musical level, across the barriers of time, in the sounding present. Despite the competency of the execution, there were times when it seemed to me coarsely melodramatic and overworked in its emotions, though I've seen my share of Samurai movies. I can't really say I was perceiving correctly. The fact is we have almost no way of judging such a performance, except as a wash of theatricalized or operatic experience. We are beginning to see more of that in recent stagings. There are those only too ready to leave it, as they say, to "gut reaction," but my guts tell me that such reaction is suspect.

I could possibly allay my insensitivity by simply letting the sounds play over me, accepting them as sonic images, closing off my mind to the projection of meanings which, on the face of it, often seemed simplistic. I'm not saying that they were, only that I couldn't tell. Were a single recognizable word to have emerged from the (for me) more or less undifferentiated sound, there would be immediately another problem, which comes from the referential power of language which, even in the impressive visual flux of Wilson, resists being fixed as image. Nevertheless, at the performance I am speaking of, it seemed clear that audiences had become attuned to letting things float over them, going with the easy currency of non-meaning, the result of which is that they are losing the capacity to struggle with a dense text in their own language.

That was also verifiable at the festival, by default, since there weren't many events with anything like a dense text to struggle with. It is another aspect of our adaptation to what is increasingly becoming a world made one-dimensional (as Marcuse observed) by the multiplicity of unexamined images. I do not pretend to anything more than an earnest reading knowledge about Japanese Noh drama, which apparently has a recondite language inaccessible even to connoisseurs, but my guess is that from the perspective of such a form the thing we were seeing was *kitsch*. As it was, the audience watched Yoshi and Company with reverent attention, not because the work was critically distanced but mainly because it was (granted the competence) exotic. That part of the festival was, indeed, for tourists. It is the New Theater's equivalent of that tradition in the commercial theatre that led, also with high degrees of skill in performance, from *Teahouse of the August Moon* to *Fiddler on the Roof*. It's of course possible in our own language to have words that appear not to mean anything, and not only in the musical theatre. And it is true that we find certain high theorists, like Julia Kristeva, who seem attracted to the "musication."

The connection of language with the nature of theatre is, despite the play of surfaces, more than skin deep. The reason is that language can be only metaphorically fleshed out—the more subtle the language the more difficult to give it even metaphorical flesh. The immemorial incantations on the air ("the complete, sonorous, streaming naked realization") that Artaud spoke of is also a reflexive mathematics of gesture ("an inexhaustible mental ratiocination, like a mind ceaselessly taking its bearings in the maze of its unconscious"), immaterial. Language ran into trouble in the theatre when the ratiocination ceased in the animated material murmur and the words were dematerialized because, at bottom, they didn't seem to count. The body may have been there, stark naked, but the mathematics wasn't. Thus, as we continue to seek higher states of consciousness, a deeper community, and—as with the ethnopoetic shamanism of current acting theory—the one undivided aboriginal reality, we need to think more effectively about language, especially now that we're not trying to abandon it.

That really can't happen, because language won't abandon us. That's the significance of what the philosophers, linguists, analysts and anthropologists are telling us when, like Shakespeare in the sonnets (a virtual manual of acting craft, perhaps the best one ever written), they say we are written, that the writing even precedes the sounded speech which was there in the beginning, before writing supposedly appeared. Here is a sample of this powerful realization in the instinctually theatricalized thought of Jacques Derrida who, along with Roland Barthes, is having a very strong influence on some of the best young directors in the French theatre:

> . . . the alleged derivativeness of writing, however real or
> massive, was possible only on one condition: that the "original,"
> "natural," etc. language had never existed, never been intact and
> untouched by writing, that it had always been a writing. An
> arche-writing . . . which I continue to call writing only because
> it essentially communicates with the vulgar concept of writing.
> The latter could not have imposed itself historically except by the
> dissimulation of the arche-writing, by the desire for a speech
> displacing its other and its double and working to reduce its dif-
> ference. If I persist in calling that difference writing, it is
> because, within the work of historical repression, writing was, by
> its situation, destined to signify the most formidable difference. It
> threatened the desire for the living speech from the closest prox-
> imity, it *breached* living speech from within and from the very
> beginning. And as we shall begin to see, difference cannot be
> thought without the *trace*.

This arche-writing is like the text behind the texts of theatre, an invisible writing, into which (the prison-house?) the Ghost withdraws, after
speech. Its concept (not the thing itself) can only be invoked, by the arbitrary ordering of signs (what Artaud saw in Balinese theatre, with its
mathematical meticulousness of gesture) and a sense of difference, as a
trace. But as with the power behind a performance, "It is that very
thing which cannot let itself be reduced to the form of *presence*."
Which is to say—in the metaphor of my own group's process—there is
only the *ghosting*: "the nonpresence of the other inscribed within the
sense of the present. . . ." Remember me, says the Ghost (who is after
all only an actor, with his own history of living speech), withdrawing,
the words echoing in the tablet where, even if scratched in the actor's
blood, the speech is only the shadow of an appearance whose identity is
suspect.

There was much experiment with speech in recent years that tried to
break down such appearances by sounding them out, a kind of vocal
decoding of dubious words, or worn words. There was also experiment
with words in remote languages, like the Greek and Sanskrit that Peter
Brook used in exploring the Promethean myth, on the assumption that
there was something behind the words, in their very *characters*, ap-
proached as hieroglyphs, that could be deciphered by the pure voicing.
The theoretical labors, in literature, over the signifier and the signified
were carried out in the theatre in the diaphragm and thorax, the gristle
and muzzle of the actor's body, "the language lined with flesh," pro-
viding the model for what Barthes said of the reading which writes

aloud, "a text where we can hear the grain of the throat, the patina of consonants, the voluptuousness of vowels, a whole carnal stereophony. . . ." In the column of air breaking open, through the sounding, the expulsion of an originary speech. More than that, the pulsional incident, the elemental *act*, from which the words were made.

What comes back, however, in "the life of a sound" (Serban's term) is the disguised recycling of the barrier language inscribed within us which, unconsciously, informs the Greek or Sanskrit by means of which we hope to escape it. So, too, the nonsense syllables which directors had actors substitute for the too-familiar passage of a dramatic text were, like the spontaneous habits of the body, similarly familiar, a kind of shadow play of old fantasy on the tongue, going back to childhood, true, but no more unwritten because of that. What we were hearing in the exercises was displaced versions of the Freudian *Fort/Da* which, as we tried to stretch beyond it, took its toll on the vocal chords. Even the dream of the pure sensible plentitude of the phonic element is written. And it is written in the language we are born to. Which is why, in the theatre, we are again having to pay attention to that—as I will, later, pay more attention to this: The splintered vowel or cracked consonant of these experiments—sounding in the body across distances as if erasing history—is trapped within the language determined by history. The *necessary illusion* of the vocal exercises (including my own) is that we are reducing if not overcoming the work of historical repression. But the truth appears to be, even when we refuse it, that language is having the last word.

According to Derrida, the pure trace does not, anymore than the force that moves the Ghost, "depend on any sensible plenitude, audible or visible, phonic or graphic. It is, on the contrary, the condition of such a plenitude. . . ." In the formation of form, moreover, what we have is the distance from this presence-absence, "the being-imprinted of the imprint"—something like the fiery white letters of the Kabbalah, a writing on air. Or, to use Shakespeare's language about the same imprint—from a sonnet which we performed (in a recent theatrework) as a collective breathing, the words materializing out-of-breath, as if written on air, because it virtually sums up what you are seeing in the theatre:

> Look what thy memory cannot contain,
> Commit to these waste blanks, and thou shalt find
> Those children nursed, delivered from thy brain,
> To take a new acquaintance of thy mind.

The thing is you are seeing what, in the thought of play, you gave birth to in the play of thought. Those children—like the unseen boy out the window of *Endgame,* on zero ground—are nurtured into being by absence. You *want* them there. They come from the arche-writing, which would be at work in the path of the trace whether we use words or not.

There is not a gesture of performance which does not follow this path, since it is in the act of performance that we are always giving visible body to what is not-there, not only the disappearance of origin but what never disappeared because it was never constituted. How could it be, since memory cannot contain it? When we look, however, at those waste blanks (the pages of invisible writing: time out of mind), we realize that we are enacting a text in the theatre even when there is no text. What is delivered from the brain back to the mind is a sense of nonorigin, the Ur-play, the phantom or vanishing source of all behavior, every sound. It is, if it can be imagined, the source of our idea of illusion. If it can't be imagined, it is a very shallow play.

One sees this (un)grounding of behavior at a rather obvious level, in the workshop or the studio, at the beginning of any series of improvisations in whatever method—and this would be so if Derrida never existed to plague us with presence-as-absence. As I've previously suggested, the actors must first work through reflexes that are already coded, engraved in their psyches and reflected by the naturally conservative instincts of their bodies. (We call it "indicating" or, in fact, "playwriting.") Those are the clichés of behavior we recognize and wait out until, reaching some threshold of performance (better writing? the trace remembered?), they reach (back?) to we're-not-sure-what, but it's differentially there, something like origins, taking its course etc., an appearance which was always there, as if those familiar gestures which were played through (*like* a ritual) are the conditions of its appearance, which is only that.

As for the life of a sound in such improvisations, what we *hear* is a sound-image, not the sound but something *being-heard,* the structured *appearance of sound,* its materialization through the senses (about which Marx said it takes the whole history of the human race to form them). But if we are seeking the ultimate life of the sound, some hypothetical absolute origin, crossing even cultural boundaries, that's another matter, only to be reached—given where we are in history—through the scripted words of our own language, in the mind if not in a text, sounded or not. The sonnets—which articulated the widest theory of theatre we have ever known by the greatest playwright we have ever known, whose drama is the touchstone whenever the theatre is being renovated—are a formulation of the idea of sounding. In that process, it is the "mind's imprint" which is being read out. That would suggest that the nature of the sound returned to time would depend somehow, as the sonnets imply, on the quality of the mind—which is itself shaped by attitudes toward language.

Some minds are convinced, like Ezra Pound, that, as you can't do it all in one language, you can't make all languages sound as if they're one. It's the difference between presence and presentness. You can have a Chinese character and a dollar sign side by side, as planes in relation, or linked by an ampersand as analogues, but there's a problem, as there was for Pound, when you dissolve them into each other. Pound—who anticipated the synchronicity and polyglottism of our vocal experiments—wrote in the *Cantos:* "In nature are signatures/ needing no verbal tradition," but added, with meticulous attention to each syllable, "oak leaf never plane leaf. . .," having sounded at the top of his voice, in the antique theatre at Siracusa, in order to demonstrate to Yeats that "English verse wasn't CUT." Well, it is and it isn't, as Pound knew, struggling against the slippage, and when Shakespeare writes, in the always-beguiling elisions of a duplicitous voice, "When I do count the clock that tells the time," even as the click of the monosyllables is liquefied by time in the telling and, "borne on the bier," moves more sonorously among its wastes. As Hugh Kenner observes, we are joined to each other as to the dead by continuities of speech as well as flesh; but in commenting on the language of the Provençal poet Arnaut Daniel, whom Pound translated and emulated, and whose poems *are* cut, he also pointed out that "A man who begins a song with the phonemes *autet e bas,* or puts *prims* between *entrels* and *fuoills,* expects us to take pleasure in the separation, not the blending of syllables, and in sound relieving, not prolonging, sound."

When the words seem dead, there may be reason for prolonging sound like a lamentation, in order to release the concentrated poem that is, etymologically, in every one of them; but after a period of such elongations in the theatre the elisions of words either didn't produce the poem or turned, more recently, into the solipsistic reverberations of solo and autistic performances—precisely the opposite of the lost universal community that was sought for in the soundings.

In the distinction between separation and blending, there is—as we know from the life of Pound—not only a theory of poetry but a politics, and a judgment as to how, through the scrupling integrity of language, society should be ordered. "With usura is no clear demarcation." Pound made his bad judgments despite his linguistic vigilance, but he did know that, aside from our inability to abandon or "get outside" language (which now seems genetically written in our DNA), we go at risk even in thinking we can, because language remains the one human activity which undeniably socializes, and most cohesively in its separations. It rejects the purely solipsistic because it abstracts. Even when it is dedicated to particulars, as in Japanese or Imagist poetry, language abstracts. It does so when The Living Theater tries to turn all sociology and psychology into a nameless chant; so long as a single word is heard distinctly through the blur of sound, the litany is returned to the dictionary and the metonymic order of time.

Language abrogates the singular in its essential nature. In that, it resembles the theatre, which is also abstract. In his essay on Artaud, Derrida says that everything that can be said of the body can be said of theatre. Everything that can be said of theatre can also be said of language, and the reverse. (Shakespeare was again being precise when he had Hamlet speak of "the abstract and brief chronicle," keeping form in history.) Like language, theatre is subject to the temporal and the impure. As a form, it is not easily controlled, because of the vulnerable human presence.It is more often than not contaminated. And like language, like all social organisms, it goes through phases of seeming exhaustion.

All said and done, not only do words count, they count all the more when *we* are exhausted. When we try to drop out of social reality, they keep us anchored. Fallen into the world (if the myths are true), they are historical accretions and keep us attached to history, in history. When we turn from words to things to block off history, we do it with words in mind; so we might as well "*Say it*, no ideas but in things," as Williams insists (though the emphasis is mine), "rolling up the particulars." The words demarcate an order of being arisen from long usage. They memorize us. Without them, we literally forget who we are. Among the delusions of the period not entirely past was the idea that such forgetfulness might be desirable. It was the idiocy of the Identity Crisis. So the titillations and exacerbations of quick apocalypse and ecstasy. But such transcendencies (as opposed to those of language) are short-lived, and when we come back to earth, the only one we know whether or not we know ourselves, we descend like fallen angels with words upon our tongues.

I am referring to what occurred in the theatre during the sixties and the seventies, not only because it's a period undergoing reëvaluation, and remembered for its sensations, but because, as I've said, the theatrical animus of the period has been appropriated by theory. The anti-verbal experiments of those years or the inventions of a new language, like Brook's Orghast, were the products of a sense of language *in extremis*. It had much to do with the identification of language with institutionalized behavior, as well as the rotten rhetoric of politics, which all the truth-telling after Watergate hasn't improved. It was bad enough that words were worn down from overuse in the natural tenure of history. But one knew also about the political seaminess of words, the scum of rhetoric, like the clogged pipes in

Genet's brothel, where the revolutionary is a plumber. (That he should turn up at Watergate hardly seems a coincidence.) In the twentieth century, where language is mass-produced, the words were contemptible with ill-usage. There was certainly sufficient reason (there still is) for not believing a word that came out of a politician's mouth, but that was hardly the fault of the word.

What was lost in the abuses of language during this period—both by those who continued lying in it and those who thought they would stop the lying by forgetting how to use it—was the continuity of a tradition which sees exactitude of language as the sustenance of integrity. The falling away from language was to begin with misguided; at its extreme, it was ethically irresponsible, as if language can be exempt, literally, out of this world; or as if you can be in this world, significantly, literate without language. As the reactionaries gloat, we now see the results in our schools.

I am not speaking of the audacious experiments we have seen in the twentieth century to rejuvenate the language by dislocating it into meaning. In the poetics of contemporary literature—the heritage of Symbolism—there have been remarkable efforts to use words as if they have no meanings, or no definite meanings, no one reliable and inarguable *gloss;* to use them precisely as if they had been obscured, long before usage exhausted them, by the wastings of time (like the inscriptions on tombstones) and the separation of word from thing; as if indeed there were no thing specifically signified by a word but only a network of half-understood possibilities grown arcane and, to rational explanation, unavailable. That is probably the major tendency in poetry from Mallarme and Rimbaud through Rilke, Pound, Eliot, Stevens and their followers. In prose, Joyce's *Finnegans Wake* is the dazzling arcanum of this tradition, which in postmodern writing, *écriture,* has led to a reversal, the opposite of gloss, *mat,* lack of lustre, subliminal seductiveness or specious mystification; instead of the valorizing sheen of reflections, an artful flatness, low-gloss, like a value-free space to be filled in, like a haiku, still in the tradition of Mallarmé, what Barthes admired in the Japanese empire of signs.

The poem's existence, in this tradition, was meant to be wholly linguistic. The whole system of intelligibility was to be contained, without reference, in the poem itself—and now in the act of interpretation—words playing off words as if the vocables and phonemes built from sound out of long experience of things to which the voice gave utterance were being dismantled into nascent sound all over again, adomically (a Joycean word), acquiring meanings out of internal resonance alone. But the words were there, luminously. They were not merely fractured or discarded or abused into parody, like comic cartoons of themselves, though there were cinematic disjunctures in the structures, which were later brought to a coarser edge of parody. But in the modernist tradition which persists in the postmodern, meanings were *disinterred*, through a system of insurgings, rather than merely disintegrated.

But to return to the vocalizations of recent theatre practice: about the time that Artaud was becoming a kind of dogma in the experimental theatre, the voice had already become a mission in conventional theatre, especially in the United States where, under the aegis of the Method, the actors were mumbling. When they tried to do Shakespeare, they were out of their element or losing their voices. In England, where they had heard Shakespeare so long they could't hear him anymore, the more seminal directors were after another kind of speech which would open up the words to fresh interpretation. The respective needs met as if in mid-Atlantic in quest of the white whale, in the idea of sounding. Suddenly, the vocal exercises were full of disjunct vocables and wordless chant. Artaud contributed a new demonic fervor and a hieratic style to the investigations, a sense of being attached to the Orphic Mysteries. Probably the most famous production to come out of the exercises was Peter Brook's *Orghast*, performed at Persepolis in 1971.

The actors were guided by Brook to explore, as Serban—who assisted him—put it more recently, "a sound which grows and turns into a cry." The sound itself is to be nurtured by a tonal consciousness which is transcultural, below the level of differences. If the actor has the courage and is willing to dare being led by the existential data, the sound may be followed back to origins. By taste, smell, sweat, the actor spirals back through the sound as if through the double helix to the genetic structure of being. There is "the immense pleasure of bringing to life very little known vibrations and energies." The meanings that arise are independent of any semantic content, nor are they the meanings of a structured music. They are, rather, the music of a soundless source, what, as Brook says, "is really human, the real substance of life." The emphasis is on "hearing" the sound for the first time, searching every vowel in a word, every glottal and fricative, for its affective genealogy.

The advantage of an ancient language—such as Greek or Avesta (the liturgical language of Zoroastrianism) or a fabricated language of elemental sounds (what sounds are not?) such as that invented by the poet Ted Hughes for *Orghast*—is that, according to the theory, it eliminates the inhibiting factor of information to be transmitted, the conceptual blockage that comes from one's own language. The idea is to move through the audial nerves directly to the primal animal brain. Without the impediment of a conceptual meaning, the actor goes right to the center of the word, to original impulses and rhythms, short-circuiting etymology, linguistics, archeology, as if being were the interior of the sound, as in the Marabar Cave of *Passage to India*. To arrive at this state, the body is tuned. The sound reveals images. The images vibrate, becoming breath, gesture, movement. That is the ethos and the promise of the theory. We all did it, more or less. With varying degrees of "commitment," "courage," "risk" (words we were all using, off the impetus of the existential), all sorts of groups were attempting to unseal the hidden content of words through similar experiments with sound, dissolving the words, like reversing history, in a reverberant reach to the timeless.

It was an illusion of impressive dimensions. I suppose there's no real way of assessing what went on in the timeless zone of the deep structure of the period. What is clear, however, is that if concepts can be short-circuited, they also follow after. The writing is always there, on the walls of the cave, the enthralled and vibrating body. All languages are barnacled, including body language. Even an invented language is a kind of conceptual prefab, as Hughes had to admit in acknowledging that the early versions of *Orghast* were dominated by the north of England Anglo-Saxon Norse patterns of his native speech. (The impact of Hughes' own poetry comes from his *not* trying to throw off the accumulated value of that heritage—whatever else is in the poetry that comes from a wider, or more culturally diffused, consciousness.) Hughes and Brook are both undoubtedly very gifted men, but their theory leaves a lot, literally, to be desired. It is dubious to say the least that a made-up language is going to be more searching or supple than an existing language. Any language has to serve its time in order to acquire, never mind subtlety, but plain force of apprehension. What gives a mantra or a liturgy its power is long ideological grounding (or ungrounding); not the absence of concept but its awakening or articulating presence—meanings interiorized by long praxis, though the earliest melismatics may have arisen on the wings of conversion or painful revelation. *Orghast* was coming at it from the other direction. But the true impact of a liturgy requires a cathedral full of doctrine. It is mere wind without it, as I suspect the chanting was, however impressive it may have seemed ascending over the landscape of the Eternal Shah, at the height of mere sensation. If it was redeemed at all, infused and interlaced with other value, that came from the skeletal remains of its Promethean myth, another writing.

Existing languages *are* accretions. That is their strength. If you are going to speak across cultures in some volatilized kinetic way—sound leaping the abyss in some coherence—you might just as well activate a living tongue. This might no longer need saying except for the recurring allurements of ethnopoesis and, in theatre, the new operatic momentum of musication. Every now and then, we do see a performance animated by a foreign language that does translate with considerable force. But there is still, in the performance, an internalized structure of understanding (quite paraphrasable, that heretical word), guided by language, that strikes down the barriers of dependent thought. The images are alive with the words by which they were moved, even as they move the words that move them. There are periods when it seems necessary to scrape the accretions off words that are made stale by repetition in familiar contexts. Sometimes we shift the context to re-enliven the words. More often than not, however, we need to scrape the accretions off ourselves, including the platitudes about the failures of language and the inhibiting dangers of concepts. Perhaps *we* need better concepts.

We see that everytime actors have descended into the life of a sound, as in the birthing rituals of the polymorphous sixties, and come back still mouthing abstractions, with perhaps a little more perversity in the hollowness. The linguistic and conceptual resources of our own language (as Brook and Hughes well know, and *Orghast* was best justified as a route back) are enormous, enlivening, almost beyond us—the slipping and sliding and decaying with imprecision also adapting, mutating, and surprising us with possibilities. But the words not believed in to begin with are not going to be believed. And the effort to do without them on misguided theory may injure even a true inquiry. That was conspicuous in Brook's international troupe when, after years of research that led after *Orghast* to their journey through Africa, they returned to the Brooklyn Academy and did improvisations. It was as if, conceptually, they had gone nowhere. And if recent versions of some of that work have improved, one might expect that after so much time, and the same might have been accomplished if they'd never followed the sound to the heart of darkness, for there was nothing that unusual about the work.

Concepts also require courage. If it's risky, as Serban says, to follow a sound "beyond one's accustomed realm of habitual expression," it may be riskier to follow an abstraction (think of Nietzsche) to its critical limit. "What is really human, the substance of life," is not by any means, conclusively, below the level of language. It may very well be *in* language, or made more substantial *by* language, the life of the sound vibrating in the body being a function of the life of the word emanating from the mind. It's not a simple division. The body is the book. In the beginning was the Word. Between those declarations is the history of thought, seized by the body, and the history of action, throwing the book at you. With variations on the themes, we are left with the haunting ontological question that pervades contemporary thought: what *was* the beginning? The revealing lesson of the experiment with Orghast is that—because it was an invented language—it was finally *less* elemental than the languages refused, the ones the actors from different countries already knew, which bear with them, along with the fossils and encrustations of habit and custom, the pulse or primal force of the originating cries and calls. That pulse or force which "drives the green fuse through the flower" is behind every good phrase or poetic line we ever encounter, even when quite abstract, like "infinity's fierce fiery arrow red," or almost unimaginable, like the stain on "the white radiance of eternity," or, coming down to earth, the casual flocks of pigeons that make "ambiguous undulations" as they sink, or, approaching the old drama of moral behavior, "Th'expense of spirit in a waste of shame/ Is lust in action"; or, on the surface prosaic: "The best lack all conviction, while the worst/ Are full of passionate intensity." If the deep structure exists at all, it is already there.

We are told that Orghast began to insist upon a grammar. That was a foregone conclusion. Despite Hughes' austerity, it was introduced in forms recognizable to the actors: present-participle endings and future tense; and rather soon at that, because they couldn't make certain distinctions without it. As for the later experiment, the effort to communicate with natives in the African bush, Brook's group rolled out a carpet and performed simple narratives in simple language. They could very well, however, have performed Shakespeare for all the natives knew of what they were saying. It would have been just about as fascinating. The actors were after all exotic, not unlike the Japanese troupe in Baltimore, speaking ancient words.

The experiments with language, or its absence in sounding, were an aspect of the desire for wholeness. They were part of an attempt, now highly charged in theory, to reappropriate from the disguised mechanisms of power the disenfranchised and divided subject of the "libidinal economy" (Lyotard)—deliverance to be achieved, with an infusion of Marx and Freud, through ritual and play. While the radical frenzy has abated, the fascination with ritual continues from the politicized sixties. As we see in the anti-oedipal bias of postmodernism, there is still the desire for the perpetual present moment that theatre seems to remember from unremembered time—the repetitiveness of ritual and the gratuitousness of play.

It should be apparent from all I've said that I'm not concerned here with the normal conduct of theatre in conventional modes of performance. They also continue with impregnable unawareness of such experiments or—as fashion and the media appropriate innovation almost before it has been conceived—a new acquisitive alertness. There is something to be said for the stubborn resistances of convention and the versatility of its adaptations, but to the degree I've suggested that here it's at quite another level in other territories of the mind. I have been alluding to the work I most respect and which, whatever the faults of which I'm critical, will be—if the theatre continues with any prominence—what will eventually determine its course. Nevertheless, the best that can be said for the addiction to ritual even through the period of minimalist reduction is, so far as I can see, that it has turned our attention back upon the history of theatre. About that, in the American theatre, we had been woefully uneducated. It has also turned our attention to other cultures, where ritual forms persist more organically, though they may be making their last hieratic or ideographic stand against the threatening imminence of westernization in the Third World.

Otherwise, the appurtenances of ritual in recent performances have been either antiquarian, pretentious, or downright foolish, and I can't imagine what social claims can be validly made for the callow ceremoniousness of most "ritual events." What also persists, I suppose, is nostalgia for the community which ritual requires, and which ritual may sustain, though it is almost nowhere to be seen. There isn't the semblance of any real structural (never mind financial) support for a ritual theatre of any scale in a society of over-vested interests, whose ceremonial occasions—if they have any scale, like political conventions or the Rose Bowl parade or Sunday morning evangelism over the tube—we are likely to scorn, unless we admire them in Pop or parodistic self-defensiveness. It's only in a non-existent or disempowered community that we can have such a plethora of dispossessed ritual occasions as we have seen, recently, in the accumulation of solo and private performances which extend, in a loose network of fraternal desire, from the more or less convivial lofts of lower Broadway to the more or less secret apartments of Eastern Europe.

Ritual desire is itself a continuation of the unexamined gullibility of the sixties about the freeing up of the libido—a legacy which now has, as might have been expected, not only more theory but a conservative reflex, in the puritanism of the born again. Actually, the assumptions behind "desublimated sexuality" and, in the liberation of language from itself, the (necessary) defense of the obscene were to begin with more conventional than they appeared. What was considered radical in the theatricalizations of life-style was more often than not part of the fantasy life of bourgeois culture, as well as the common stock of honorific sentiments attached to human sexuality since the Enlightenment—that ceaseless discourse about sex which was, as Foucault has shown, far from being restricted. It was rather sponsored avidly through the nineteenth century and to the present, as a function of the social and mental operations of power. That text became part of what Victor Turner has called the "tolerance of discrepant forms" reflexively mirroring the advanced stages of capitalist liberal democracy. We see the platitudinous side of it in the current tradebooks of sexual encounter and the proliferation of post-Gestalt therapies where the old genital fixation gives way, often through theatricalizations of repressed desire, to the ontological breakthrough of the clitoris and the more invaginated and polysemous pleasures.

The same impulses occur as something more than platitude in, say, the byzantine intricacies of new literary theory, with its feminist and psychoanalytical adjuncts, where the idea of play has become, in the ingenious occultations of desire, something like a miracle drug. But while the omnipresence of play may be extended *in theory* through an infinite field of deferred pleasure, in theatre as in life—where the real estate of desire is *time*—play is amortized. No matter how we disperse the old plot or deconstruct the framed stage, there is only the *illusion* of a continuous present which may, in its own occulted forms, suffuse the processes of play. Instead of being, then, a wasted agency of undirected stimuli, libido is summoned in the suffusions—by what Freud described as an essential appropriateness of the mental structure—to "an appropriate alteration of reality," as in the critical theory of Brecht, who could also make his adaptations. Although he was outwitted, in the theatre, by the illusions he was denying, he outwitted, in life, the political order which paid for his struggle through the contradictions. It's as if he had derived some life-preserving sense from the very duplicities of the form which he resisted. The illusory process is *time-serving*. There is no alternative. Yet that's something to be learned and not assumed. Every radical advance in the theatre has come from another illusion first subverting and then impacting the one before, in order to prolong the dominion of play. But there is something in the play-within-the-play which refuses even that, as when Lucille—in Buechner's play on precisely this subject—cries out against the Revolution: "Long live the King!" It is the most libertarian moment in the play. So, in the language of the unconscious, repression is the ground of social and political action, as well as new possible forms of gratification, putting reality in the subjunctive as the subject keeps shifting, but within the unshakeable declensions of time.

It is that other dominion of time—what memory connot contain, though very much on the mind—which theory has wanted to thwart in confiscating theatre to its purposes, or letting itself be seduced by theatre. It's as if the dream-content reappropriated dream-thought in the incessant interpretations of the play-with-the-play, reversing the analytical process. We have seen, in theory, virtuosities of performance that seem, indeed, to be playing to its limit the theatre's entrancing concept of life as a dream—forgetting that, in theatre, it's really a conceit, a proposition to be tested in the *acting out;* and that, in theory, the theatre always pulls back at the speculative limit, on the ontological cliff's edge of illusion where, it appears, all language fails. So far as current theatre is concerned, it remains to be seen whether it has lost the capacity for the language which can bring it to that edge. It is a condition which would seem beyond politics, or prior to it, and so it is, that waste blank, the sublimity of the moment—to which the theatre must commit.

It is not, however, quite the same moment we have been *drawing out* in the recent serializations of our new theatre which, in the aftermath of too much politics, seems to be playing through a rather arbitrary plenitude of disjunct images a kind of ruined destiny. It is the reverse image (or illusion) of a future without end—or, without the right word for what it defers, an aphasic, agitated, ruminative, cyclical, and futureless facsimile.

Precipitations of Theatre:

Words, Presence, Time Out of Mind

●

Ah, yet doth beauty, like a dial hand,
Steal from his figure, and no pace perceived;
So your sweet hue, which methinks still doth stand,
Hath motion, and mine eye may be deceived.

(Sonnet 104)

THE CUE IS LYRIC, BUT A PREVIEW OF THEATRE—THIS SURREPTITIOUS
anxiety teased out of us by words. There is an incitement of action in
the insidious motion, a play of mind that will not hold still. What we
see in the quatrain is enlarged on the stage, as if the dull substance of
the flesh *were* thought. No sooner thought, it may leap to the quick in a
conditional passion: "If beauty have a soul, . . . If . . . If . . ."; thus
Troilus, "publishing a truth" of Cressida, that "inseparate" division,
admitting "no orifice for a point as subtle/As Ariachne's broken woof to
enter," and with another knot of fanatic reason the whole truth shattered to untruth, "fractions of her faith, orts of her love,/ The
fragments, scraps, the bits, and greasy relics/ of her o'er-eaten
faith"—like an inflamed Derridean rehearsing the *bricolage* with all
the dazzling garrulity of unspeakable desire.

"O madness of discourse,/ That cause sets up with and against
itself," constructing and deconstructing. It is one of those self-
enamored scenes of double watching "That doth invert th'attest of eyes
and ears,/ As if those organs had deceptious functions. . . ." The
Shakespeare canon is full of cautions: "scan this thing no farther," says
Iago, that seminal figure in the theatre's solipsism, whose very

character is a testament to the duplicities of the form.

We may think of Iago as an avatar of difference, an undoubted presence leaving origins behind. The scene is now familiar, slipped, dissolved, and loosed; yet is there not something within us, as if another Troilus, that doesn't want to believe it? What *will* hold still, for all the seeming? That's the problem to which we keep returning in the theatre, which suffers from a repetition compulsion, the neural itch in the concept of rehearsal—for which the French have the right word. Despite improvisation, the unnegotiable demand: *répétition*. But: what is there to repeat, except the repetition? By whatever name, it is related to the in-terminable debate over *mimesis*; that is, what is being presented or represented? and was that a good idea to begin with?

When Plato took up the problem in the Cave, he knew by instinct that it had something to do with language—the difference between words, things, and the appearance of things. He was not, we know, too happy with imitation. Aristotle took over the problem in the *Poetics*, speaking of the faculty of imitation as an instinct, "natural to man from childhood, one of his advantages over the lower animals being this, that he is the most imitative creature in the world, and learns at first by imitation." Poets are poets, he says, not because we call them such, tacking on the word to their meters, but "by reason of the imitative nature of their work," through which we learn, "gathering the meaning of things. . . ." Still and all—to the degree the world now seems to be made out of language—what we gather and how we gather it is also problematical, if not altogether meaning-less, the slippage of signifiers amounting to a loss. According to the doctrine which denies itself as such, words appear to be part of the same exchange mechanism in which we can say, as we can of language, money is no object. (As for beauty, now an absence, "how will you find beauty," as William Carlos Williams puts it, "when it is locked in the mind past all remonstrance?") We are now likely to think, along with the poets and semioticians (whose reasons may differ), that poetry is words about things that wouldn't exist except for the words.

If so, the question remains: what is the nature of the existence of the words? In the theatre—which Plato thought was up to no good—the bodily presence of words becoming unbodied complicates the problem:

In the erotics of theatre, words are (theoretically) corporeal. They are up there for public scrutiny. The mind's eye echoes the mind's ear. Words act. They are elements of the scenic investiture affecting, synesthetically, light space rhythm pattern sound, but they also re-sound at the deepest level of the *mise en scène*, through self time memory consciousness as well. Mere words, true. Problematic to the last breath of being. The material elements of theatre—like the body itself—situate us. The abstractions I have named are the diaphanous substance belonging to the genotext, both overdetermined and elusive, accounting for the expressive ambiguity of the event, whether or not there are any spoken words. To be aware through light space rhythm pattern sound that self time memory and consciousness are there (or shadows of them) is one thing; to *say* those words, or others like them, in a theatre event is to reify the amorphousness of the thing until, in a scandal of knowing (like the words of a ghost), it virtually hangs upon a breath.

Words on a page may be conceived of, as Roland Barthes does, as "pulsional incidents, the language lined with flesh," grained with voice, "the breath, the gutturals, the fleshiness of the lips, a whole presence of the human muzzle," carnal, libidinal, "throwing, so to speak, the anonymous body of the actor" into the ear. But that is "bliss," the wish fulfilling of "writing aloud," which Barthes has to confess is more attainable at the cinema, where speech may be amplified like a closeup, granulated there. The appearance of words in the theatre is at the same time less mediated and more strained, if not estranged, never so blissful, though words issue from a voice in a palpable body. But there's the rub, they may stick in the throat. Even the recurring technical problems of the voice—the actor's major liability on the stage, what goes first when he is distressed (the hurting voice may be doctored for the screen, or soundtracked later)—suggest we're never entirely sure what the issuing involves, except that in the theatre the voice itself is at issue. It is ironically germane that during the last generation concern for improving "vocal production" in American actors so they could perform the rhetoric of classical roles has led, through the advent of psychophysical exercises (Grotowski, Brook, Wilson, etc.) to the emergence of the abstract "vocal image" so they could act in "theatre pieces" with fractured roles or without roles, outside of Plot, apart from the psychology of character, in the purer concussions of sound and motion, more or less grained, wordless (for a while engrailed by the anti-verbal), carnal.

The words are returning to the theatre like displaced persons. But in rediscovering the dissociated power of voice unconstrained by the old conventions of role or text—with a short-lived politics to the impulse—we tended to forget that not only the voiced self (concealed in but impelled by the body) but the voice itself (as alien to the body as a soul?) is already an image, worded, *before* it is heard; that is, subject to the interior "writing" which (we're now told) precedes speech. That something of the sort occurs is verifiable in the improvisational work of actors. It is meant to be liberating, and often is, but inevitably passes—with or without words—through a phase of banality and cliché, the reflexes of old writing in the body, before exhaustion, boredom or unexpected stress turn up intimations of the originary trace. As for the voice, to speak of its appearance is of course metaphorical, though there is a pulsional incident, no pace perceived. The voice is an ideograph that is invisible—part of the apparent materiality of theatre by which the eye may be deceived. Even before it appears, it is already *sounding*. The trouble is we're not really sure where it comes from, no less the words when they issue forth. Even with knowledge of the mechanisms of the voice, its functioning—thoracic cavity, larynx, glottis, the sinusoidal motion of acoustical velocity—all we know is that something comes up through the nervous system which is incommunicable and disjunct, bereft of flesh once it escapes the body, muting the body plaintive as it goes, all the more as it escapes into language or—in the annihilatory vision of Artaud, pulverizing words— *"metaphysics-in-action. . .* , the truthful precipitates of dreams. . . , a sort of animated material murmur in the air. . . ."

As Artaud describes it in the Balinese theatre, "after an instant the magic identification is made: WE KNOW IT IS WE WHO WERE SPEAKING." Perhaps so. In the Western theatre, we've never been quite so lucky, we're a lot more indecisive, or *equivocal*. About the nature of identification, degrees and nuances, whether you do or whether you don't (a dilemma even to Brecht), who is speaking for whom—and the metaphysics that goes with it—there is something in our theatre that keeps us guessing. Whether we should guess or not is at the center of the arguments over representation. Nor am I convinced—though there may be less argument in the Eastern tradition—that it is generically different in the Balinese theatre, for all the ecstatic and exquisite account of it given by Artaud, summoning up in our own theatre, for a while, instant versions of the hieratic, along with archetypes from Jung. It may be true, as Artaud declares in *The Theater and Its Double,* that "in their perpetual allusions to secret attitudes inaccessible to thought," in the eminently vivid play of the Double's terror, arising from the inarguable automatisms of the unconscious (valid for Artaud, without differentiation, in all cultures), "in the human as well as the superhuman the Orientals are more than a match for us in matters of reality." The evocations are certainly chastening. I am persuaded—from having seen other forms of theatre from the Far East—that there is a superior instinct for the perdurable, a scrupulous attentiveness to stillness, the spiritual petrifications of motion, a glossary of apparently repeatable signs "in the close and subtle web of gestures, in the infinitely varied modulations of voice, . . . and in the . . . sonorous interlacing of movements." But somehow, in the "monstrous aviary" of performance, in "these strange games of flying hands, like insects in the green air of the evening," there is a "sort of horrible obsession, an inexhaustible mental ratiocination, like a mind ceaselessly taking its bearings in the maze of its unconscious"; and this obsession like the unstopped motion of Artaud's own mind, as he describes it elsewhere, whipping his innateness at every striated nerve-end of thought because of having lost the key to that other language, "and this kind of irritation created by the impossibility of finding the thread and tracking the beast down. . . ." And suddenly one remembers, in the precipitous desiring of the *"gestures made to last,"* the equally terrifying reverberations of that fleeting image in a host of words, the awful irreparability of Ariachne's broken woof.

After which—about what the theatre shows, or can show—we are forced to suspend judgment; which may be, in the self-recursive epistemology of the theatre, what the theatre has shown us from the beginning (or since we've been conscious of it—what?—*as* theatre), even as it forces us to make judgments ("What, has this thing appeared again tonight?" [*Hamlet*]) about the seeing and the seen.

How do we know, in the theatre? What do we know about the theatre, through the theatre? What are its origins? and what is the nature of its presence? What is it *now, as it occurs,* breathing and being breathed, as it is, before the eye? what is it, then, in the mind's eye? in the confusions of eye ear and the other senses? in the synesthesia of its perceiving and the being perceived? To what does a performance refer except to itself?—and what is the ontological status of *that other thing* if what is there is not the thing itself?

"Now, mother, what's the matter?" As theory about theatre the unanswerable question which starts off the Closet Scene goes to the heart of the matter, more literal than meets the eye—in this drama of inexhaustible questions about an absence which is, so far as we can see, the subject of the theatre itself. One of the functions of the theatre, it is commonly said, is to *make present.* But—returning to the question almost impossible to keep suspended—make *what* present? And where does it come from? and in what order or dimension of time?—whether it be, as Aristotle says, an imitation of an action in the form of action or, like the Ghost, some other substanceless substance or actionless mode of being, suggesting a higher reality which is, whatever it is, *not* theatre. In this matter, where fathers fail, mothers are also unreliable.

What we take to be real, to be sure, is often in contrast to something we consider less real. The frames can shift, and what was unreal can suddenly seem real, with the shock of recognition or a more or less fine suddenness. We are constituents of the shifting, vulnerable to time. The reality we refer to in the theatre, does it exist before or after the fact made present? in the performance? and is the fact that is a fact an activity, an activity of mind, or a state of being? and did we put it there in the act of perceiving? or was it there before we looked, hiding or withdrawn, ready to come when, like Faustus, we say the magic words or, like the Balinese actor, make the hierophantic gestures? or—in the absence of a trusted text or sacerdotal glyphs—having to be dragged kicking and screaming onto the stage like some of us (what *is* stage fright making present? for it's there in every performance, is that the Double?), even at this belated time, into the twentieth century, where the problem of perception and the problem of the real—like the structural relations of self time memory and consciousness—are pure vertigo?

In the profusion of neo-ritual theories of theatre (Richard Schechner, E.T. Kirby, David Cole, etc.), the implication is that we are returning some mystery to being, *re*-enacting, giving body to an absence by an "actualization." In these theories, there are nuances in the attributed substance of actuality, but there is agreement on this: the theatre event functions as a mnemotechnic sign that returns to "life" something that is, for the time being, out of sight and is, for the time of performance, once again embodied and manifest. The existence of this other—wherever it happens to be when the performance is not taking place—is assumed (though sometimes unassumed, when the performance is conceived of as a second genesis). It exists, like the orthodoxy of an absence, at some numinous remove, whether or not anybody represents it in history; or, if we get nervous about needless attenuations of the unbodied transcendental, in a beggar or a manger, or a madman at the liminal edge of thought—as in the equivocating empiricisms of myth and poetry. We may think of it as Sacred even if we are secular, with something like the still unresolved mixed emotions we have in front of a Renaissance Crucifixion. But even there, we know it has had to be profaned to be perceived.

Since we are talking about the unimaginable, something other than the Imaginary, there are many convolutions. Perhaps it is more like this: that it *once* existed, or still exists but inexplicably withdrawn (like the God of the Kabbalah who endowed us with the void), or never existed, but in some mysterious way occurs as a *first thought,* as in the aboriginal myths of Origin, a bringing of something that never was into the world, out of a void a stone a thread a laugh. The motive behind the manifestation is indeterminate, maybe gratuitous, and the substance of it unpredictable. What appears to be true is that there is a privileged space in reality that wants to be filled. There is an African folktale, for instance, about the spider Ananse who brought blindness into the world because the god Wulbari wanted *something.* The point seems to be even subtler than what Troilus had in mind when he saw too much.

Whatever it is, however, that may be elsewhere or otherwise, we cannot apprehend it unless it bleeds into the body of performance, not necessarily (anymore) like Troilus' passion, "In characters as red as Mars his heart/Inflamed with Venus"—but with a minimum materiality which, no sooner there, steals (or is stolen from?) the figure (by the act of perceiving?). At that level, we're in the vicinity of that palpable diminuendo of presence in the depreciating sequence of Beckett plays, the mimesis of dis-appearance. Whether Sacred or profane, "Something is taking its course," the substantiality of which we can attest to even if we can't explain it, and even if, like Freud, we not only keep a rational arm's length from the Sacred but dematerialize the profane. Thus he writes, in a 1911 formulation of mental functioning, trying to define as plainly as he can what the "unconscious" has come to mean "in psychoanalysis and in psychoanalysis alone":

A conception—or any other mental element—which is now *present* to my consciousness may become *absent* the next moment, and may become *present again*, after an interval, unchanged, and, as we say, from memory, not as a result of a fresh perception by our senses. It is this fact which we are accustomed to account for by the supposition that during the interval the conception has been present in our mind, although *latent* in consciousness. In what shape it may have existed while present in the mind and latent in consciousness we have no means of guessing.

What appears in the theatre, however, appears (as if) *remembered* "as a result of a fresh perception by our senses," although one of those perceptions may very well be the felt difficulty, described by Freud in another essay, of telling apart unconscious fantasies and actual memories which have become unconscious, either of which may produce neurotic symptoms. "One must . . . never allow oneself," he warns, "to be misled into applying to the repressed creations of the mind the standards of reality; this might result in undervaluing the importance of [f]antasies in symptom-formation on the ground that they are not actualities. . . . One is bound to employ the currency that prevails in the country one is exploring; in our case it is the neurotic currency."

In our case, it is the currency of the theatre, which may be neurotic to the degree that it presents or represents what may or may not be fantasies—the elusive line of demarcation being whether they are there *as* actualities or *as if* they are actualities (some new theatre events being very indecisive about this distinction), though it may be another actuality altogether that we are talking about, not a fantasy but an *anamnesis*, with all the estranging materiality of a *déja vu*. So with the playing out of the desire for origin or source or primary being: what might be felt as a radical discontinuity in experience is remembered as an elsewhere or an otherwise which remembers back. There is something in the memory of theatre which suggests that even the numinous shares the longing, as if it would claim its own: if there is a wandering soul, it seeks the earth, the home of love—*the specific gravity of an elsewhere in a destined place*; thus Oedipus at Colonus or, in another dimension of being or non-being, those dispossessed figures on the mountainside in the Japanese Noh, from which Yeats borrowed, because he was attuned to, the tactile dreaming of the bones. Or, in his *Purgatory*, the way he irradiates a remembered image which is a virtual signature of the ancient form:

> Study that tree.
> It stands there like a purified soul,
> All cold, sweet, glistening light.

With darkness around it, and in the window above, in which—as in the Closet Scene—the mother's pollution will be replayed: a scene whose replications, like a mirage, correspond "to a parallel symbolism in the mind, a deployment of ideas and appearances by which all that is theatrical in the theatre is designated and can be distinguished philosophically." The voice is Artaud's in a more cognitive vein. "If in fact," he says in his essay on "The Alchemical Theater," "we raise the question of origins and *raison d'être* (or primordial necessity) of the theater," searching for "the essential drama, the one at the root of all the Great Mysteries," we pass from philosophy back to poetry (the millenarian voice returning:) to a subtlety so rigorous in its intellectuality, "an acuteness so intense and so absolute," it might open an orifice where none seems to exist, to the same radiance which, failing in Cressida, illumined Yeats' tree:

> *but with drama*, after a meticulous and unremitting pulverization of every insufficiently fine, insufficiently matured form, since it follows from the very principle of alchemy not to let the spirit take its leap until it has passed through all the filters and foundations of existing matter, and to redouble this labor at the incandescent edges of the future. . . . in order to rediscover in solid and opaque form the expression of light itself, of rarity, and of irreducibility.

For Artaud, the true theatre is born through the turmoil of the Cosmos, "out of a kind of organized anarchy after philosophical battles which are the passionate aspect of . . . primitive unifications," the subliminal in the sublime. What is important to understand, when we think of his scourging all Western drama, as if *he* were the Plague, is that the cruel theatre of alchemy is meant to contain "the essential principles of all drama, already *disposed* and *divided*"—the amnesia from which the theatre suffers, forgetfulness forgotten, cut off from origins—"not so much to lose their character as principles, but enough to comprise, in a substantial and active fashion (i.e., resonantly), an infinite perspective of conflicts." What he, and Derrida, seem to obscure (Artaud somewhat less) is that, if there is really to be an infinite perspective of conflicts, the Theater of Cruelty cannot be *without representation*, making itself "the equal of life," which Derrida, in the essay on Artaud, defines as "the nonrepresentable origin of representation"—immediately after saying that the Theater of Cruelty "is life itself, *in the extent to which* [emphasis mine] life is unrepresentable." So, *some* of life appears to be representable, and how could it not be if, according to Artaud, we are going to have a theatre *with drama*, the form in which difference counts?

It is true that, to the degree our theatre has labored to construct an infinite chain of representations, a version of life *totaled* by mimesis, merely "doubled and emptied by negation"(Derrida), packaged in falsifying characters, "false, false, false!"(Troilus) as the words which fly up to heaven while thoughts remain below (Claudius) emptied in dialogue and psychology, Artaud has wanted to make the theatre a battleground on which imitation would be destroyed. When, however, on another battleground, Falstaff plays dead, he puts an end to that illusion, or—if not an end—a limit which demands that the double illusion (the false character playing false) take its place in the infinity of perspectives. The same may be said of Artaud's conception of an essential drama to be materialized "in the image of something subtler than Creation itself, something which must be *represented* [again, the emphasis is mine] as the result of one Will alone—and *without conflict*"; among the unifications being a sort of meeting of East and West, leaving us with the problem of discerning, as we do in life, which representations we believe, which we prefer, and which are possible in this world.

As for Artaud's apparent attack upon words—while it is wrong to deny the fierce ambivalence, similarly directed to the body—what he is after is a form of theatre which "permits the substitution, for the poetry of language, of a poetry in space which will be resolved in precisely the domain which does not belong strictly to words." This domain, with its surcharged and abstract spirituality, not only recalls the underworld of the Orphic Mysteries which "subjugated" Plato with their moral truths, but "that nostalgia for pure beauty of which Plato, at least once in this world, must have found the complete, sonorous, streaming naked realization. . . ." Another fantasy? or the theatre's fondest imagining, intrinsic to the form, the unfalsifying remembrance of the representation, seminal, genetically coded?

Is it there, in the play? that question. What else can one say? it *must* be there, in the play, for how else would it be remembered? It is not only that, for those who remember, the theatre remembers, but there is an *urge* in the mode of memory—whether that other thing exists or not, was before or never was, can still be or not, still, only a dream remembered. There is a sense in which we do theatre today, in this secular age, like a bride and groom before an altar, having composed their own ceremony, yet reaching to an Image through the solitude of their vows (the unspoken skepticism sounding), performing in the purest shape of their desire, having to *say* it as if in the beginning there *was* a Word, as we now realize we must do to interpret the dream.

There is a similar desire in the "public solitude" of the actor—what Stanislavski taught—reaching out to the unfathomable through the filters and the foundations of a calculus of objective detail, the existing matter of the "given circumstances," as if desire could be perfectly articulated, and the Will refined, through the anatomy of specific action into *belief*—much as St. Ignatius does in the *Imitatio* of his exercises, which resemble nothing so closely as the famous Method. It is no wonder that actors have learned much from devotional systems. The lessons have been absorbed within the tradition of Realism as in countervailing styles of theatre. Where the method is memorable through the performance, there has been a meticulous and unremitting attentiveness to the *de-conditioning* of the body's coarseness (to think of it as Yoga does) into the materialization of an Idea. We are also taught to follow the course of a particular in a privileged space. To imagine Golgotha for St. Ignatius is not far afield from imagining Clov's kitchen for Beckett, ten feet by ten feet by ten feet—where, unfortunately, he stares at the wall, the rage for order not unlike Artaud's, seeing his light dying. "Mene, mene? Naked bodies?" Hamm taunts him with the biblical handwriting. For the actor, the play is a virtual manual of craft; for the theorist, an encyclopedia of deconstructionist thought. If well acted, it is astonishing in the concurrence of method and madness, if not meaning, maybe that too ("We're not beginning to . . . to . . . mean something?")—the intense *specificity* of what is there and not-there, a negation not empty because devout. So, when John Donne says in a sermon that "the Holy Ghost himself is figurative," the Doctrine of Real Presence may seem to waver (something stealing from the figure) but through the realization of His *intention* in *that place*, "a progresse house, a removing house here upon earth, His house of prayer," as impeccably located as that place on the ramparts, removed *to*, where that other ghost, profaned, will speak across the abyss to his son, *and not before*—in both cases penetrating to the structure of credibility (in the theatre? in the world?), as well as assuring, in His house as in Elsinore, the "credibilizing" (Coleridge) of the Ghost, though He may be doubted after he speaks.

The thing is that even spirit needs a local habitation, if not a name, a *topos* or situation in history, through the intercourse of body and word. Sense data alone—even the freshest perceptions—will not reproduce the absence or bring it into being, although the senses may prepare the ground. The theatre, like Donne's removing house, is a memory space. So, in the technique of Stanislavski, it is *sense memory* which, by triggering belief in the one small truth of a particular action, may cause an actor who doubts his own truth to recover it within the structure of a role, thus attaining faith in the reality of the entire play. There is a charismatic complexity in the notion of the one small thing. A daily ablution or an exercise or a precise physical detail may key, as a reflex of mind, the credibility of a performance. Or it may be—like the hovering fly in Dostoyevsky, a boot or carrot in *Godot,* the button of King Lear or the faithlessly pledged sleeve of Troilus—the ontological pivot on which the ultimate reality can turn. It may also be, the one small thing, a mote in the mind's eye, ghostly—no more than a word, that metonymic thing of difference, ceaseless, catastrophic, Iago's fig, or the nothing that comes of the nothing in Cordelia's choice; and as we pursue the idea/thing we may feel, as Hamlet does, that we may not be spirit at all, but moles at best made radiant by desire (words words words) only by desire, sweating in our senses (perception after perception) and, as in the cellarage or Kafka's Burrow, battering our heads, sensing, through the ground. The final place is bound by the law of gravity, that irreducibility. We "give birth astride of a grave," says the blind Pozzo. Is that the repetition we were waiting for, the end of seeming? sightless, or the Eternal Return? More of the Same or yet another, whichever it is the theatre makes *that* present—*along with the subjunctiveness of the prospect,* if, if, if, the unregenerate doubt of doubt, doubting—, bringing *its* Image into reality, what we take to be life.

When the theatre is distinguished from other arts, we usually hear of "living theatre," or the interplay of actor and audience, but these undeniable banalities tend to disguise the one inalienable and arcane truth of theatre, that the living person performing there may die in front of your eyes, and is in fact doing so. The other perversity of theatre is that somehow we want to watch it happening, or the imitation that seems to conceal it. "The house is being watched," says the Madame in Genet's *The Balcony,* where the mirrored fantasies played out come to their exquisitely negated consummation in the Funeral Studio, mirror of all mirrors, a mirage. *Who is watching whom?* Not only are the living encircled by the dead, as Marx said, they seem to be constituted by the circle—in that sense, but more subtly than Gertrude knows, "Passing through nature to eternity." It seems to have been the prehistoric condition of theatre to have formed a circle around that circle on what was considered sacred ground. "Heaven and earth!/Must I remember?" But in the act of memory there is an actualizing force. What appears to have been forgotten imparts a virtue to what is, even when, as in Genet, it is remembered perversely. "I reconquer a domain," says the Bishop, still carried away with his performance, after he has stepped down from the cothurni. Undressed, exposed, *the most ordinary of actors*," but with the absurd residue of a "solemn stiffness!"—excited by the prospect of an erection, like Beckett's tramps at the thought of hanging themselves from the tree: "Final immobility. . . ." (It was never guaranteed that desire would be anything more than grotesque. Yet the eye may be deceived:) "I beleaguer a very ancient place from which I was driven. I install myself in a clearing where suicide at last becomes possible. The judgment depends on me, and here I stand. . . ." Thus, Bishop, gasman, actor, and the person-who-acts conflate at the dreaming end of the scene (is he still acting? who?) into the mock-apotheosis of desire, lustrous, masturbatory, a near-bodiless self soliciting a self, "the most tender and luminous sweetness . . . , a charity that will flood the world. . . ." You can almost believe it, the sonorous, streaming naked realization.

Like the ripenesss which is all. "And that's true too," says the blinded Gloucester to the apothegm of his Bedlam son. He is at the edge of the battleground, after the miracle of his self-deluded suicide from the cliffs of Dover, spared by "the clearest gods. . . ." Whatever they may be, it was again, as with the Holy Ghost, a matter of placement. One imagines the action on the cliff—in a drama which has shattered all ritual—as if it were done immemorially, origins reversed, the father grounded in the son: "Set me where you stand." Precisely, like a sacrament before the fall. And . . . and, what's true is true, but the most appalling truth comes right after the acknowledgment of ripeness, when Lear and Cordelia are led off to prison, like God's spies, to laugh at gilded butterflies, and: "Howl, howl, howl!" the laugh laughing at the laugh, cutting the brain in an infinity of perspectives, sonorous streaming naked dumb.

One wants to move the unmoving in order to be moved. Life did not precede us. It is the form of our energy in creation, humbled, given up in passage. Life is what we do not take with us, and yet it goes with our going—and that is somehow painful; sometimes, as in *Lear*, painful beyond belief. (It can hardly be matched, even when remembered, as with Edward Bond's version of one of the savage daughters gloating over a torture she'd like to inflict on her father: "Look at his mouth! He wants to say something. I'd die to listen. O why did I cut his tongue out?") The legacy persists in the unstopped wounds, reticulated scars and self-reflexive circuits of the play within the play, where it all comes back, as in the unconscious—"Is not this something more than fantasy?"—, the eternity of the problem: the Image of the theatre going its tautological round.

For it's not as if there's theatre and then the mystery—even if there was once a Mystery and then theatre—as if they exist sequentially or in separate dimensions. The theatre is—whatever its origins—part of the Mystery, involved in its perpetuity and transformations, like the leopards entering the temple in Kafka's parable, to become part of the service. What they bring into the temple is unspeakable. In that strange, and strangely repeated, ceremony, in which the leopards drink from the chalice, time is if not cancelled, spilled. We do not know if it is moving backwards or forwards or in any ascertainable fashion at all. It spreads over experience like a radiance, or a stain. Though unspeakable, it is not silent, it makes a continuous sound, phonemic memory of the first cry? the susurrus of history? prophetic voice of the wide world dreaming on things to come? or the immutable echo of that howl? What we hear—confronting each other, desiring a meeting, not knowing what we see for all we hear—takes us through the detours of thought (what, in the dreamwork of Freud as in the studios of Genet, is the memory of gratification) to the emotion experienced almost before time, by The Watchman in Argos: a dread that the apparent silence will never by broken or, in "the rumor and outcry" of flame, that it will. The murmur of time is the essence of the theatre space, mantic, coded by history, precipitant, or concealed, an *aura*—as if the voice we hear in the sounding, almost forgotten like a bereaved self, is the distraught voice of a god, whose true body even the gods have never seen:

OSIRIS: How good it would be if one god could see another!
ATUM: My face will look upon your face.
OSIRIS: But how long shall I live?

". . . and Atum—protect/protect from all gods from all dead. . . ."
Or, dismembered source and inaccessible final cause of the cry:

(ACTION): THE ANIMAL IS SLAUGHTERED, ITS MOUTH FALLS OPEN UNDER THE KNIFE.
ISIS: (*To Thoth*)
    Open thy mouth—
    the Word!

Among the confusions of time are reversible habits of thought. Thus: the cunning of the present! how it tries to *mis*represent us, coming to us as we come to it, as if we stepped out of a mirror—instead of in. Anxiety is a race with the future, as if death came out of the past. We live by leaps and lapses, fits and starts, in a dream of fluency. Inertia is the memory of matter. The sounding of time—what we say to ourselves within ourselves, the language of inwardness—is not of *our* time. That disjuncture, and the reversals, are relevant to what we perceive in the theatre, *what-is-there*, the thing we make present by whatever means. As regards the past, one of the principal issues of the theatre is how much of it is locked; that is, how much of the past is past.

So much of modern thought—disturbed by a world impeded (if not made) by words—wants to free language for use *now*, as if names were (or should be) only referrable to present things. That is why there has been so much experiment with the denial of names and the refusal of words, as if now is (or should be) all the reality there *is*. So, among the early modernists, even the past had to be present now—no *pre*-tense, not as a fiction, a representation, but a living reality—for how else could it be and we think of it? And if it weren't (the reasoning going thus:) it couldn't *be* thought, as if memory were the fiction. Indeed, in the line of thought descending from Freud and Marx through French Structuralism, what is remembered is the forgetting, a displacement, which has to be deconstructed to reveal what is there, not *as* revelation, but as the simultaneous existence in the mystifying word of the memory and the forgetting. In the classics of Modernism, that simultaneous existence was the object. We move through our heads like time: what was is there, now, *in situ*, here, placed—like Tiresias becoming Ezra Pound: "Who even dead, yet hath his mind entire!" That achievement, like Eliot's presentness of the past (yielding to Revelation) in *Little Gidding*, is like a sounding within a sounding, a near-miracle of language arising from its failure (like Gloucester's suicide) or, depending on the degree of your positivism, a shell-game of words held up to the ear.

In either case, something still plagues us, a sense of what-it-was, accomplished, elsewhere, otherwise. Too much of the thought past *feels* just that, *past*—sometimes a disjuncture, and hence unavailable, forgotten or remembered, whether as repression or illusion; and sometimes, *as* memory, not at all dead or impoverished for *not* being here, except for the memory, *in* it and *for* it. What is here, then, is *another* thing, also accomplished. (The Japanese Noh, a palimpsest of remembrance—studied by Yeats through Pound—apparently means Accomplishment.) Its thingness is a function of the thing remembered, available so, *no sooner remembered*, as though it had never happened before (what it was there, *then*, enigmatic), and of course it hadn't—since it couldn't be now if it had. Exasperating as they are, these revolving tricks of memory, intrinsic to the language, are also inseparable from the idea of performance, which at some liminal margin of mimesis is trying to embody, or re-member, what it is that is going out of mind.

Forgetfulness is not involuntary. The memory we don't want is the memory we don't have. Memory doesn't merely lapse. A lapse of memory is an act. What *did* happen? What *was* done? (We can see in political amnesia, like the quick forgetting of Vietnam, that there is more than mere absent-mindedness involved.) From the beginning, theatre has been concerned with the action of memory, trying to remember a beginning. The convolutions of memory are engrained in the form: What we never forget is often what never happened. What we always remember is the evidence of what we've never done. So, memory is the desire of the not-accomplished, the reflex of desire itself, which is located on the stage of being at the limits of consciousness—the theatre in which all things come to be, dreaming still.

"This prophecy Merlin shall make," says the Fool in *King Lear*, reciting what *ought* to be, "for I live before his time"—and soon he disappears, unexplainedly, from the play. For a while, we don't even know what happened, or that it has happened. It's severely troubling when remembered. What are we to think? The line about Merlin has already juggled time. The business of prophecy is the remembrance of things to come. It is history doubled over: told in advance, so that it *can* happen and be re-told. But what *is* there to be told? That word, too, is like a knell. The stories we remember, out of time, take us seriously, almost more than we care to remember—which is why we can hardly tell some of them anymore—or forget—not as they were. How we remember will determine what we do in the theatre, and how we do it. What happened to the Fool? He appears to have served his time, as the chatter of an absence. Is that all? Is the Fool's life a prophecy or a duration, that which ends because it can't be anymore? He is gone before we know it, an elision of presence. What has that to do with us? "And thou no breath at all?" The heart sinks, as if through a trapdoor of inwardness, the dream of fluency bottoming out: a dead space in time?

The fact is that something is slipping away. Fact is slipping away. The theatre confronts this fact, like the loss of the privileged figure which is always privileged, the vanishing of the difference which makes sense. Of course it is only an appearance, or so we want to believe. "A fact historically understood," says the Russian Formalist, Boris Eichenbaum, "is one which has been withdrawn from time. In history there is never any repetition, simply because nothing ever disappears but only changes shape." So Lear, with the dying Cordelia, lamenting his Fool, gives us a cue for believing what we maybe want to believe, that the two of them are somehow one. So? In a moment they will both be dead. Is there a further change that can redeem them? The Russian thinks there is, as if history can save us from art, which took its cue from history. "Never, never, never, never, never!—" Poor Fool. We are once again at the limit of theatre, time's negation of time. We turn with relief to undo the button, the one small thing on which reality still turns, like Gogo emptying his shoe. It's not what the Russian meant by history. But even art can't save us from art. It's as though we are back at the beginning, as if it had all been remembered, a bad dream.

"We that are young/ Shall never see so much, nor live so long." Maybe so. We seem to dream the same dream. That's part of our history. Some have made the argument that it *is* our history. What do we make of it? In our time, there seems to be no prospect but beginnings, a mere circle of origins, interpreting the dream, always looking for a sign. As with Krapp's spool or Didi's round about the dog in the kitchen, we become aware that, to make a beginning, the beginning must be begun again, each round more radical and disturbing, with all the insecurity that brings. "Something has ended/ And what's beginning is still blind," says a socialist woman in a play by Heiner Müller, heir of Brecht, sophisticated by Beckett, living still behind the Wall. The play is called *Cement.* Here, the dialectic of the dial hand's seeming is politically tortuous, as we can see in this exchange near the end of the play:

> IVAGIN: We can't stop history the way we stop
> A horse, just anywhere it pleases us.
> We won't make it within humankind
> But what is needed here is cement.
> POLYA: You don't need to tell me where my place is.
> (*Opens the window. Sirens.*)

About that, like Brecht, Müller must be equivocal. The rest of us may appear more fortunate but we are all now indoctrinated to beginnings, displaced, often denying it but wanting to be told.

Between Müller and deconstructionist thought, there are sympathetic reflexes which, all told, amount to the subtlest semblance of an orifice in a wall of ideology, as there is between East and West (both kinds). As for humankind, and its supporting doctrines, we are now advised that it is a representative figure of that already-dispersed language in the interstices of which man was invented, composing a self—a subject of receding origins in an unthinkable space—which might not be collectively possible. Whether we can make it, then, within humankind, now that "the imperious unity of Discourse . . . , situated within representation," has broken down, what can we say except that even the profoundest of those who doubt it, like Foucault, can offer little more than a subjunctive that wants to be an imperative, the always-insufficient rhetoric of desire:

> *If* those arrangements were to disappear as they appeared, *if* some event of which we can do no more than sense the possibility—without knowing either what its form will be or what it promises—were to cause them to crumble, as the ground of Classical thought did, at the end of the eighteenth century, *then* one can certainly wager that man would be erased, like a face drawn in sand at the edge of the sea. [Emphasis mine.]

That is the last paragraph of *The Order of Things*, that formidably asseverating book in which the disappearance of man is virtually guaranteed but remains, at the ending, something like a wish fulfillment, while the marginal persistence of the forms of representation force us to a deeper apprehension of the reflective origins and subversive powers of theatre—now so dominant in consciousness that it is beginning to appropriate the ungrounded Discourse, becoming the Image of our thought, so that the act of reading the writerly becomes rehearsal and performance, a "deceptive plenitude" on the edge of vanishing, producing meanings in the infinitude of play.

If play, in the potency of gratuitousness, is an incursion of mind breaking down the tyranny of the Cosmos, there is a representational instinct in the Cosmos, it would appear, that seems to be calling the tune for "these angular and abruptly abandoned attitudes, these syncopated modulations at the back of the throat, these musical phrases that break off short, these flights of elytra, these rustlings of branches, these sounds of hollow drums, these robot squeakings, these dances of animated manikins" that Artaud observed in the Balinese theatre, "displacing the axis of the human figure," but never quite erasing it as, in the passage from East to West, some last cyprian redoubt of desire, washed back, refuses the accessions of the sea. Out of the fearful symmetry in the phenomena of desire, we have come to the doxology of an active forgetting. We have come to believe—in the course of thought from Vico and Nietzsche to Freud, Joyce, and Heidigger—that we are living in the wake of beginnings that are leaving us behind, unable to sustain their momentum but incessantly circling back in the replenishings of repetition, the undertow of dreams, that, seeming to conceal, also open out—to what prospect? this repetitive thought, we can hardly tell, though it seems to have something to do with the self-corrosive enshrining of repetition itself, the solipsistic over and over-ing, as in the act of acting, trying to remember with compulsive specificity, like Troilus: "Instance, O instance": the breakdown and reconstruction of truth.

In the dreaming body of the actor, the living image of the displaced person: self time memory consciousness desire. The theatre is always beginning over, that's the trouble. Where do we start? It's clear we have work to do, *now, as it occurs*. But: there is always one thing to be remembered, the eye-opening consequence of the one small thing. We look incredulously at "the promised end" (*Lear*). Can we make a beginning of that?

Theatre and Cinema:

The Scopic Drive, the Detestable Screen, and More of the Same

●

"... For they are dead, and I ... I ... I ...."
Virginia Woolf, *Between the Acts*

SOME YEARS AGO I MADE A SERIES OF FILMS, WITH ED EMSHWILLER, FOR a theatrework I was directing. The films were projected on a large planked wall, white-washed, and suspended by two ropes from the flies. It was the only scenery for a sort of Brechtian fairy-tale about a funny old lady who was really a murderous witch and who, at one point in the play, pursued her good daughter and her soldier-lover in a mad chase around the theatre, going in and out of sight until, as she was about to catch them—a lethal butcher-knife raised in the air—they veered suddenly at the wall as if to smash themselves upon it in a suicidal marriage pact and, miracle of miracles, ran right through the wall and into one of the films. The mother flourished her butcher-knife and went high-tailing after but, as the scrambled tale was told, bounced back ignominiously to the floor. It was a crude but, if I must say, rather nifty piece of stage trickery. The wall was designed like a Chinese puzzle box, triggered like a pinball machine, with a number of swinging doors and windows which figured dazzlingly in the ensuing confusion, and confusion of realms: stage and screen images pursued and combined with each other, splitting and substituting, overlaid, in displacements more bewildering than the Czech Camera Obscura, or the *mise en scène* of the unconscious. In the supersaturation of appearance and disappearance, the scopic drive was driven to distraction. Meanwhile, back on the floor, the wicked mother was dazed and the lovers were escaping on the film when she picked herself up and—as if to crack the barriers of all forms, a true apostle of Mixed Media, postmodern—went hell-bent at the wall, bang, like the utmost subject of desire, the desublimated apotheosis of the Nietzschean Will to Power, pure manic aggression, after them into the film. And they all disappeared down a road into a perfectly regressive dissolve like going backwards with Derrida down the Originary Trace.

It wasn't the first time—this rather total reinscription of the theatrical space in the cinematic image—that I'd been involved in a literal assault on, or ontological confrontation with, the limits of a form. Sometimes, it seemed, we wanted to do away with the space entirely. In the late fifties, for instance, I had directed the production of *Waiting for Godot* that, while it had other things to recommend it, first achieved notoriety when it played at San Quentin, the first theatre performance at a maximum security prison since Sarah Bernhardt had been there, early in the century. It was the production which gave a groundbreaking anecdote to the Theatre of the Absurd. But the barrier-breaking that concerns me now has to do with a disjunct moment in the play when Gogo with not the faintest idea of what he's doing there or where it all began or what happened yesterday or a minute before ("I'm not a historian," he says later)—frightening himself to death for no reason at all, which is reason enough—suddenly turns from Didi's plot-making futilities and with the full force of his desire to leave the repetitive structure of this dreadfully self-reflexive play, strikes the proscenium arch a great blow, like Samson knocking down the pillars of the Philistines, crying out for all the estranging world to hear, "I'm hungry!"

The hunger is visceral, psychic, formal, metaphysical, paracritical—the actor's desire meeting the character's desire meeting the theatre's desire (my own desire at the time) for liberation from its own limits. The blow was not actually in Beckett's script, but the violence surely was—as it was in the actual rage of the actor (and my own rage) against the predicament of an estranging profession which kept him nearly starving (he is eating now, and in the movies), and our theatre (The Actor's Workshop of San Francisco) on the edge of bankruptcy. So there was also rolled up in the actor's fist—in the unappeasable successions of desire—the distressing memory of the old logic of continuity in the theatre, of provenance and providence, the wish-fulfilling narrative placement of being, a more accommodating structure with a better story and—in this elegiac scene on the edge of nowhere, mere appearance (with a Cartesian frame around it)—more dependable conditions of presence.

Naturally, the proscenium didn't fall. Never mind the structure at San Quentin, in our theatre it was over thirty feet high pure concrete block, the unbudgeable objective correlative of a certain ordinance of power with attendant modalities of being, and consequently *seeing*, that have persisted in consciousness even when appearance was being pushed, like the rocks on Cézanne's mountain, up to the picture plane by the Sisyphean effort of modern art. If there was any secret presence in those rocks, a mysterious power to behold, it was the heroic mission of Cézanne to hold it in place on the surface. But a surface is surreptitious, and our habits of perception are stubborn. Appearance equivocates even in the upfront facet-planes of that indomitable brush until, cracking like the ice floes of *Alexander Nevsky*, the surface disappears. Or so it seems. Especially that transformative surface which Meyerhold—the great Russian theatre director, teacher of Eisenstein—called "that detestable rectangle, the screen. . . ." Meyerhold detested it because, almost as if it *were* the proscenium, which he detested too, "it can't be thrust apart"; and he understood Eisenstein's art of montage not so much as a testable proposition in a space of thought, but as the means for obliterating the rectangle from the consciousness of the spectator. But the power of the screen, that duplicitous surface, is more self-serving than he knew, insisting on having it both ways. Which is forever troubling to the demystifiers, and the pure in mind.

In the history of the cinema, there has been an equally heroic effort to overcome the duplicity, whose ideological reference is Renaissance perspective. Even before Cinerama—that naive filmic equivalent to the "all-over" expansionism of the Action painter's canvas, at the margins of peripheral vision—there was the wide-angle lens, or superimposition, or the empty frame, or the Vertovian anomalies of composition which unsex or depopulate the site of narrative so that it seems without perspective. The vanity of this filmic enterprise has, as I've suggested, its equivalent in the theatre in the determination to break down the privilege of the proscenium arch, with its recessively encoded, analogical space, and its imperial heritage of the one best seat. Unfortunately, such determination rarely has the ideological purpose or aesthetic resourcefulness of Meyerhold or the critical self-consciousness of Gogo's blow, a sense of its vanity and—so far as theatre structures are concerned—its material cost. In recent years, we have had the supposedly liberating presence of the thrust stage, that phallic substitute which sustains the Name of the Father without bringing us one inch closer to the Sacred Grove.

That delusion was part of the folklore of the Cultural Revolution after World War II, made affordable by the blood money of a permanent war economy with its Edifice Complex—all those new theatre buildings of the fifties with their adjustable platforms and multiple pre-set switchboards and pneumatic lifts and electronic turntables with their annular rings, returning us, through all the architectural fantasy, to the unregenerate Same. It's like thinking, when you're dealing with an irremediable condition, that a change of scenery will do the trick. "Actually there was a wall, across there . . . with a door," says Teddy in Pinter's *The Homecoming*, a threshold play of the period, inspiriting to a new insurgency in the theatre of the sixties. "We knocked it down . . . years ago . . . to make an open living area." But Pinter equivocates too, that's his method. "The structure wasn't affected, you see. My mother was dead." And Teddy was wrong, of course, he was an academic. The Great Mother was reborn in the Age of Aquarius, at the time of the Vietnam War. Yet, even with the participatory *anima* of the Counter-Culture, in what is still called Environmental Theatre—where you might sit or squat or move all over a polysemous space in a converted garage, or even dance (then) with the actors who, after a symbolic birthgiving, might embrace you and feed you—the one undeniable presence was the continuity of our proscenium minds.

Which is not at all to say—to put this in perspective—Renaissance minds; if only that were true, in theatre or in film, with any frequency. Nor am I convinced—though I have done much experimenting with the plenitude of empty spaces and other configurations—that we automatically have better minds when we abandon the conceptual space of the proscenium arch, or any other convention whose framing power was constructed out of history by great intellectual force over many generations. There *may* be, surely, a conception of sufficient force to warrant abandoning it, or trying to knock the bloody thing down, but we are often ingenuous or cavalier about abandoning even less sturdy conventions, like those of the dramatic fiction, which reappear, despite us, like the Allegorical Figures in Genet's *The Balcony* after the Revolution. In that scopic brothel like a movie palace—where mirror upon mirror mirrored is all the show—all the scenarios ending in death are rerun like a reel of film. Genet's homoerotic fantasies in the brothel, which are curiously chaste, like film, are surrounded by a production apparatus which is more like cinema than theatre. Yet it *is* theatre, at the teasing selvedge of the form, where we remember that there is no ontological coalescence of mirror and screen. In the theatre, the not-quite-Lacanian mirror is traditionally curtained, as is sometimes incongruously true of the blank screen.

Like the screen, the curtain is a convention worth reflecting on. It is now, in the theatre, an emblematic symptom of the concealment which, in theory and in politics, we distrust. We remember the archaic theatre when it wasn't there, but we often forget that the intervention of the curtain in the open arch was an achievement of great psychic dimension, not only as a subliminal trace of the Ark of the Covenant (though it was presumably invented by the Romans) but to the degree that what we see there is, if you reflect upon it, *better not seen*—at least in life. To want to see it enacted is almost perverse (not to mention the desire *to* enact it). "Is this the promised end?" "Or image of that horror?" Isn't that what tragedy is really about, despite the placebo of catharsis? and comedy, that cruel and skeptical form, even more culpable? a coverup, to keep you laughing, but maybe smarter for that, for to think you *can* see it may be even more perverse, as Plato thought. Draw the curtain. "Not yet!" Those are the opening words of *The Family Reunion*. Among other things, a curtain takes pity—though we've been distrusting that emotion too, like the family, like the oedipal presences of the originary narrative, in recent times. A convention, like an emotion, may seem exhausted, but it certainly begins to wither when we stop imagining what it was like *before* it was there.

Try that with the curtain, not yet conceived of as a theatrical gesture. Think: the first impulse of intervention, somewhere between revelation and duplicity: *now you see it now you don't*, the generic difference that becomes the living subject; and then the difference between the curtain rising and the curtain falling or the curtain split and parting, or drawn from one side of the full length of the stage, stage hand seen or not, or the Kathakali half-curtain, where the actor's legs and headdress are seen, but not the torso, that strange anticipatory presence, like the three knocks behind the curtain of Molière, or the rolled curtain of a play by Yeats, with an Image on it (borrowed through Ezra Pound from the Japanese screen); or a curtain such as we once constructed in San Francisco, which swagged way above the audience, its underside satin and royal blue (for Brecht's play about Galileo, who had his troubles with perspective, as Brecht did with the shiftings of history around the Bomb), released into space like an unfurling sail and, when it closed the proscenium again, became a movie screen, framed *outside* the proscenium by discordant images of Vitruvian man, putting the perspective in perspective by somewhat cartogaphic versions, *on* the screen, of the accelerating half-lives of subatomic particles and the shrinking time of interplanetary space, where the nanoseconds beyond film seem as if they *were* filmed, by Paul Sharits, or as if a landscape by Michael Snow were being dissolved—out there, as we are told, where there are no curtains and space folds back upon itself as if Creation and not film were being reversed, and all matter is turned into *foam*; or, finally, the curtain we used for a second production of *Godot* in a smaller theatre, a sort of tat-tered assemblage, de-eroticized and see-through, which rose halfheartedly and never made it, falling feebly to the ground—as if the phallocentric universe had given up.

"Let us pray," says Hamm in *Endgame*, whom we first see curtained, black specs over blind eyes, as if *in* camera; who seems at times like a theory of film, which "is the first art form," as Walter Benjamin said, "capable of demonstrating how matter plays tricks on man." Film is also the medium in which all the things of the world may be *appeared to*, without (as for Hamm) the residual certifying presence of living things. That, I take it, is one of the things that Michael Snow was attempting to demonstrate in *La région centrale*, that there would be something more than a qualitative vacuity in a universe without anything human or even animal, uninhabited, except for the residual perceiving. If, as we're also being told, the human presence is a poverty in the space of life, film seems to have the capacity to impoverish it even more, to a thing among things that merely appear. In any case—and whatever the state of the human—film at last makes possible the accomplishment of the notion that a rose may appear red to a stone. The existence of film helps to clarify Whitehead's notion of *prehensions*, according to which "all actual things are subjects, each prehending the universe from which it arises." The darker side is that it sometimes feels like a dead universe, repeating the singular first person: I . . . I . . . I. . . . By contrast, phenomenologically, the theatre is full of *ap*prehension. The verb is voiced. The stage is filled so that it may be silenced. The curtain falls. Or, as in the *Kaspar* of Peter Handke, there is the definition of a precipitousness in the form: "What is/ worth striving for is a curtain that/ is just falling."

Lévi-Strauss says of structure that it is a virtual object whose shadow alone is real. But what can be said of a structure which—the further it is traced through the corporate body of our cinematic apparatus (a body without organs)—seems like a shadow's shadow? It's a strange shadow, indeed, which has the look of something that is looked at, as the theatre doesn't, and can't, no matter how many times it has seemingly been seen before, since it has never been seen like *that*. The theatre's duplicity is of another nature, the bodily *presumption* of a presence that disappears. Meanwhile, let us realize—the curtain parted or fallen to the ground—that there are fecundating options on that ground where, as Derrida says in his essay on Artaud, "each agency is linked to all the others by representation, in which the representability of the living present is dissimulated or dissolved, suppressed or deported within the infinite chain of representation," as if, however, that were a scandal, and I suppose it is. It is also, and I suspect we must live with it, the most perversely obsessive subject in the theatre, what makes it detestable (to Plato, to Tolstoy, to Augustine), *the subject of perversion,* what we want to see and shouldn't, in the theatre or in the living present—what immemorial wall or membrane between?—to which the theatre is always tempted but refuses, refusing to live on anything but its own terms.

Sometimes the theatre refuses to live, even in the theatre. It is a form which knows the presence of self-corruption only too well. It is a time-serving form, and I shall return to that. But its terms can be very powerful, seductive and seditious, and may impel other forms to the living present, as with painting in recent years (also in disrepute) after realizing that not even the purest abstraction could achieve relief from representation, which simply can't be painted out. After Pollock stretched the canvas into an action field like a stage, the canvas itself was assaulted, its shape and materiality, like the proscenium arch. Even in the barest minimalism the imperiousness of the paint was eventually scorned in favor of the carnal body or purer conception, as if acrylic were elitist, as film—which can do without the body and was always expensive—must inevitably be with the price of silver going up. In the confusion of realms, and economics, it remains ironic that cinema, so fabulously profligate, should retain its populist dimension, though even its revolutionaries should have known, in the days of its silence, that to the ordinary person in the chain of representation, money talks because, as Marx showed, it is almost wholly empty, like the filmic illusion, onto which can be projected the sum of all desire, its low degree of existence invested with dreams. Which is, as Metz and others have pointed out, what makes it "real." (After the vitality of its infancy, cinema went through a period where old men, running the industry, were making the stars; now the baby moguls work upon our dreams with the inconceivable Force of galactic millions.) With money, as with cinema, it appears, subject and object are happily married: you can have anything I want. We shall come back to that lucrative subject in a while.

As for the activation, or appropriation, of the other arts by performance, certainly it was important for the pictorial enterprise, equivocating there or itching for action, to come off the wall, as in Happenings or Body Art or other hybrid events, as it was for the theatre, feeling stifled behind the proscenium, to go into the streets. But mostly the exercise was rather like jogging, the returns not yet in, questionably beneficial, and in any case neither the picture frame nor the proscenium seems to have been really exhausted (no more than fiction, according to the recent recantation of John Barth, who had written a famous essay on "The Literature of Exhaustion"). Which may say something about the durability of the Oedipus complex against the depredations of deconstruction.

As for the detestable screen it is still very much attached to its origins in perspective, and the generic narrativity that goes with it. So long as a projector is trained upon a screen—whether or not a curtain parts upon it—the Name of the Father will be there, like the stains upon Hamm's stancher, that displaced tampax like a Veronica, despite the feminist agenda or *A Film About a Woman Who,* or whether or not it's a film made by a woman. When it's not there, there will be no more movies to go to, for the perceptual and the eidetic will have been joined, which is perhaps a consummation devoutly to be wished, but I doubt it, and I'm not counting upon it in my time. I say this despite some admirable experiments to break with or away from the screen into the seemingly truer and more nurturing ambience of a participatory space, like Anthony McCall's environments around the projecting apparatus (before, with two women, he became doctrinaire about Freud's Dora), or the video feedback performances of Joan Jonas mirroring her own body mirroring itself, or Stan VanDerBeek's unceasingly ingenuous search for a purely oneiric space, where self-actuated images are hypnopaedically projected on a geodesic dome, or the movies are shown on steam. If there is any resemblance, in the latter, to the film theorists who—like the Young Hegelians from whom Marx split with scorn—seem to be appropriating filmic experience entirely into consciousness, that is purely coincidental.

There are those in the theatre who sometimes wish that the entire cinematic institution would vaporize like that, but there is nothing theoretical about the desire. They find the screen detestable for much simpler reasons than Meyerhold. The most basic reason, to be sure, is that the cinema has been taking audiences away from the theatre since its inception—which is another (at least partial) illusion that needs to be put in perspective, taking us in other theoretical directions, but returning us to more of the Same.

If films appeal to larger audiences than theatre, that is perfectly normal and terribly strange, and they do so for two apparently contradictory reasons: they are both more familiar and more fantastic. In this country especially we are still without a substantial theatre tradition, and it's unlikely that we'll ever have one. Going to the theatre is not part of the natural rhythm of things—belated because of the Puritans, outcast like the King and the Duke, derivative and mostly idiotic until the emergence of O'Neill, somewhat embarrassing, certainly ponderous, even then, and even now—only for the most limited segment of the population (high Wasp or Middle European), in large urban centers—considered anything like a necessity of life. It is unimaginable that if we were bombed out, as the Germans were, that the first buildings to go up after the blitz would be the post offices and the theatres, as they did in German cities, although we would very well show movies in the shelters, as we do in submarines, or the "race-track" bunkers where—with the projectile intelligence of the Road-Runner—the MX missiles would be released.

As everybody knows, we grew up teething on film, and movies are second nature. Thus, no matter how bizarre or banal a film may be, it feels more credible than theatre, not only because of its powerful impression of reality, the dominion of the immediate image, an absolutism of immediacy which is more than documentary, but in the sense that it has better credentials, *more credit* (on the money market and in the libidinal ecomomy), and thus seems more authentic, if not—to use a weary old word of another era—*relevant*, even when it puts us to sleep. I am not being facetious about that, but specifically theoretical. "In all forms of society," writes Marx in the *Grundrisse*, "there is one specific kind of production which predominates over the rest, whose relations thus assign rank and influence to the others. It is a general illumination which bathes all the other colours and modifies their particularity. It is a particular ether which determines the specific gravity of every being which has materialized within it." The mode of production which Marx had in mind here is obviously bourgeois capitalism, but he might as well be describing the cinema, whose particular ethos, we know, is etherized upon that table—even when, in its earliest period, the audience was proletarian.

My own relationship with the movies started in a proletarian environment, where it never occurred to me that the signifier would be inaugurated by my presence, the production of which depended on the ubiquity of an ideological being which was not-there, transforming the world into discourse, the text of which was already written. It wasn't until I became acquainted with the philosophical groundwork of no-beginnings that I stopped walking into the middle and insisted upon seeing movies from the start. But then I also recall the prototypical days—long before I saw any theatre—when you went to the movies and wondered if there were live actors behind the screen (the enlargement of whom you never figured out), even when you took for granted that (feet sticking to the ammoniated floor) you could stay there all day and see the film over and over, the actors never getting tired.

When I do think now about the evolution of this relationship with what became the cinema—particularly within the overlapping discourse of film theory, psychoanalytical theory and feminist theory—the equivocating nuances of my attitudes seem rather accurately described (if I may refer to Beckett again) by the opening of

Molloy: "I am in my mother's room. It's I who live there now. I don't know how I got there. Perhaps in an ambulance . . ."—the ether being all-pervasive. The indeterminate voice of the narrator continues:

> My mother never refused to see me, that is she never refused to receive me, for it was many a long day since she had seen anything at all. I shall try and speak calmly. We were so old, she and I, she had me so young, that we were like a couple of old cronies, sexless, unrelated, with the same memories, the same rancours, the same expectations. She never called me son, fortunately, I couldn't have borne it, but Dan, I don't know why, my name is not Dan. Dan was my father's name perhaps, yes, perhaps she took me for my father, I took her for my mother and she took me for my father.

In any event, it is the family resemblance which is critical, and the recidivist mirroring of the unconscious, that unconscionable phase, the Imaginary. One of the significant functions of the fantasizing power of film seems to be—like dream, like trance, like the ethereal and soporific mythopoesis of Mallarmé or Bergson—to keep us sleeping.

We're still amazed by the "vacuous actuality" of film—and in the worst of films still convinced by the actual vacuity. Theoretically, it seems not to make any difference. "Besides for me," as for Molloy, "the question did not arise, at the period I'm worming into now, I mean the question of whether to call her Ma, Mag or the Countess Caca, she having for countless years been deaf as a post." And still is, of course, since you can't talk back to a screen, or touch what's on it, no more than you can bring up the vacuity in theory, which keeps deferring the subject because it's presumably nameless. Whatever was true then, the question does arise now. If something of our childhood does come back at the movies—and I suspect that has to do with *how* we allow ourselves to think about it, in view of what it *is*—there is no guarantee of its being any the less difficult or confusing than it was before—and it may be all the worse for that, our having profited so little from experience.

Either the theatre or the cinema can be the ground of an activity which is thoroughly solipsistic (as I know very well from the limiting dangers of my own work in the theatre). I see no real difference in that possibility by which the spectator might consider himself the passively organizing principle of the cinematic or the theatrical event. Depending on how you look at it, they are both apparitional and both aboriginal, but the identification with one's self that is the condition and outcome of a pure act of perception, making the viewer a tautological subject, is the result, too, of an attitude *toward* viewing in the spectator. The one who is there before anything appears to inaugurate the possibility of being thoroughly beguiled by the solicitations of the look's caress is already consciously soliciting the possibility. People less sophisticated are not likely to be looking anymore for the actors behind the screen (when we did, we were *critically* attentive to the apparatus, even if fooled), but they are also likely to be putting up a variable resistance to the discourse. This does not prevent anybody from conceding that the unhearing immateriality of film—deaf as a post but affirming the incestuous existence of untouchable objects, like the dubious tree falling in Bishop Berkeley's forest—seems more fully *there*, more overwhelming, than the palpable bodies in front of your eyes in the theatre.

We hardly think of a suspension of disbelief at the movies, whereas there is always on stage a compromising incompatibility between the corporeal body and the *mise en scène,* which includes touchable objects that seem unreal until you've made some very peculiar mental adjustments to very dubious but insistent conventions. There is something refractory in the theatre, which may be thought of—with its history of improbable possibilities and impossible probabilities—as the adversary proceedings of a real presence, which is neither so direct or *verité* as a *mise en présence.* In the theatre, credibility *is* the issue, as in foreign policy. As with the Ghost on the ramparts, the "thing" we expect to appear, so with the acting process: whatever the thing is, it is never certain, and if it doesn't appear you wouldn't believe it, and you're not sure you do when it does. As Coleridge realized, the word is perfect and indeterminable for whatever it is that comes and goes in a performance, without which there wouldn't be much of a performance, though we never trust it. The thing is that it comes and goes, and the environment of theatre is not conducive to making it seem real, in the more obvious sense of that word—though its entire history has been dedicated to that project. Against the artifice of the form, the thing doesn't stand a chance. You have to work to validate it every night. Think of the Ghost, that pitiable convention, and the now-classical conundrum of the stage, as contrived by Shakespeare: how to make it not only believable but real.

When we think of the real in the simplest sense, the movies seem to have the advantage. The documentary superiority is inarguable. There is the elephantiasis of reality in the closeup. And no theatre event—no matter how excellent the staging—can approach the impression of an eeriness being *realized* (what Malinowski, speaking of magic, somewhere calls "the coefficient of weirdness") that can be achieved by any third-rate horror movie or some aesthetic atrocity from outer space or the filmed drawings of *King Kong,* not to mention the coefficient of realness with weirdness in the seamlessly animated photographs of a movie I once saw (by Jules Engels) on the French town of Uzès, in comparison to which the mere reality of the town itself, were I to go there, might seem a hallucinatory fraud.

That real unreality of the cinema was, to begin with, the most startling attribute of the photograph before it ever became a moving picture. The great dramatists of the late nineteenth century saw what was coming, the revenge of reality on the photograph, what Eisenstein—who had worked in the theatre—tried to impede, the tyranny of *motion*, which confirmed reality by obscuring it in a form which wouldn't exist without it. The coming "attractions" of Eisenstein were episodes in film like Meyerhold's ideographic acting style, the static "passes" or, later (also indebted to Meyerhold), Brecht's *gestus*, the bracketed action of Alienation, or "the lapidary style" of Chaplin, all of which rein in pure motion for a moment, taking a breath for aim, before the whole thing runs away. (The prose of Marx was also possessed of motion, but that same holding action which we see in the swollen laconicism of Eisenstein's montage is in the staccato rhythm of this marginal note from *The German Ideology*, denotatively filmic, like a shooting script: "*Hegel*. Geological, hydrographical, etc., conditions. Human bodies. Needs, labour.") Ibsen, however, sensed that such an impedance might never again be possible, that out of the fissures of reality, like the crack in the chimney of the Master Builder, came dispossessed motion, aflame with its own becoming, which "seethes and precipitates and changes color, inside. . . ." That is Rilke describing Ibsen, "among the alembics in the firelight."

In Rilke's beautiful account of Ibsen's methodology as an alchemical quest, it's as if Ibsen were already making film, anticipating Bergman, Antonioni, Rohmer, and a hundred other filmmakers before and since, not to mention Artaud, who hated what he thought Ibsen represented. Rilke goes on to say, addressing Ibsen:

> . . . you took the enormous decision at once and single-handed to magnify these minutiae, which you yourself first became aware of only through glasses, that they should be seen of thousands, immense, before all eyes. Your theatre came into being. You could not wait until this life almost without dimension, condensed into drops by the centuries, should be discovered by the other arts and gradually made visible for single individuals. . . . This you could not wait for, you were there, and that which is scarcely measurable—a feeling that mounted by half a degree; the angle of refraction, which you read off at close quarters, of a will burdened by almost nothing, the slight cloudiness of a drop of longing and that barely perceptible color-change in an atom of confidence—all this you had to determine and preserve; for in such processes life itself now was, our life, which had slipped into

us, had withdrawn inward, so deeply that it was scarcely possible even to conjecture about it anymore.

There were always psychological subtleties in the theatre, even on cothurni and with megaphones in the mask, but it wasn't until the Jacobean period, and in Racine, that they acquired a specifically psychoanalytical passion, the desire to *see* every microscopic inflexion of desire in a form where magnification, in the acting, takes certain subtleties away, and where the eye, watching, is unassisted by magnification and can be more or less acute depending on the distance from the performance. (In assessing conditions of presence there is also what Stanislavski called the "given circumstances"—not, however, of plot, but the distancing of presence [an aspect of which he called stage charm] by the magnitude or voluminousness of the auditorium. There is surely something different about seeing a film in a vast space with a ton of velour and pendent crystal and floral scrolls and cupidons and Buddhas with jewels in their foreheads, and seeing it in a cinémathèque or a classroom or Cinema 1 of 4 in a supermarket. I'm not sure how the fantasies change but I suppose they do. Yet it's nothing like the radical variations of presence with the diminishing or expanded dimensions of a theatre, where the voice is heard differentially and appearance is altered at the most obvious physical level. Take makeup, for instance, part of which goes in the theatre as compensation for the expansion. It may do wonders for the actor—as we've seen in the stupendous makeup jobs in the movies—but only so much wonder, then, if you're close up on a hot night in an unairconditioned theatre where you can see the actor sweat, and the director doesn't want that, as Grotowski *did* in his theatre, where you were forced close to the playing area, or surrounded by it, yet formally separated by the Kierkegaardian intensity of the sweat. I have seen whole plays with the best of performances swallowed by the wrong stage as if there were nothing present, and I have seen actors dwarfed by sets or displaced by moving scenery or, for that matter, by the magnitude of an electronic score or by a careless sound operator who drowned them out or deprived them of some untellable decibles of presence by the wrong calibration of an amplifier. I have also directed in one of the world's more affluent theatres [the Beaumont at Lincoln Center], vast but deceptively intimate, but with a seating arrangement so pitched that to this day—even after much investment in making the stage more accessible to the auditorium—much of it is off-limits and an actor tends to look not only smaller but younger, immatured and a little callow, no matter how old he is. There is a whole theory of theatre in such contingencies of performance, which are, in other alarming ways, indecipherably germane to its presence. That indecipherability leads us back to Ibsen:

The violence in Ibsen's late drama came from attempting to do what seemed impossible on a stage and what film, later, could do without half trying—as it can achieve comic effects by incongruous splicing that would elude, in the theatre, the most impeccable timing of the funniest actor. What Ibsen wanted to do—at the end as in the beginning—was to bring towers and whole mountain ranges into the "capillary action" that Rilke described, and to sustain in a world which was increasingly imaged the image of a world which refused to be.

Sometimes he knew it was impossible. Thus, he located the domain of the wild duck *behind* the photographic studio, as if desire, fantasized by the living actor, could never compete with the actuality of its imagistic exposure within the dimensions of the real, which had to think of other dimensions. Ibsen was already imagining the tilting ice floes of Eisenstein when, after moving into the bourgeois parlor from the fjords and mountain tops, he moved out again and tried to bring an avalanche on stage in behalf of the invisible. Those unsurpassable late plays of Ibsen, such as *When We Dead Awaken,* are to this day dismissed or misunderstood by people in the theatre, as they were by my teachers in drama school years ago, who called them psychotic and ignored them. And they nearly are psychotic, those premonitory visions of what we'd see later on film being realized or apprehended, then, at the excruciating outer limits of theatre, as if the alchemical process of dematerialization—the apocalyptic desire of Artaud to burn away the execrable body of enacted desire—were brought to consummation in the alembic and suddenly reversed, or the specific gravity of the dream, its ether, were extruded back into flesh by sheer will.

When we used to think of life as a dream—as in much of Shakespeare or in the great play of that title by Caldéron—we were thinking of it as theatricalized; but now, as if the dream is dreaming the dream, as in "The Circular Ruins" of Borges, where the body of the dreamer is consumed in the concentric blaze of the fire-god's seeming, which magically gives life to a sleeping phantom or, when it appears that a phantom is awakened to flesh, caresses him and engulfs him "without heat or combustion"—we think of it as cinematic. There is still, behaviorally, the mimetic presentation of the self in everyday life; and we have just been through a generation that tried with some (illusory) success to theatricalize our politics, which was already saturated by image and image-making. In the media, and especially video, where the stagings occur in a rabid consumption of image, the film is more than doubled over. "Any man today," as Walter Benjamin wrote in the thirties about mechanical reproduction in art, "can lay claim to being filmed." Which is why, again—in the circular reality of the system of reproductions—we think of film as being realer.

As experienced, phenomenally, even a Chekovian play, in every naturalistic nuance, seems more artificial and more *acted* than almost any film you can think of with maybe comparable characters but a less reliable psychology in a similar setting. The "realest" Chekov I've ever seen was the film version of *The Lady with a Dog* which, as I remember, was performed mainly by superbly trained young actors of the Moscow Art Theater who, good as they were, could never seem as natural on a stage. When we reach back into the archives, we are likely to accept on film what would be forbidding in the theatre, into whose archives we obviously can't reach—acting, for instance, as ideographically factitious as Donald Crisp's in *Broken Blossoms*, precisely because it is *not* being acted *right there*, where the archive doesn't yet exist. Crisp seems to be working in another order of reality—which we're tempted to call *theatrical*—than Lillian Gish who, despite the assumed mannerism of her crippled gait, seems a natural. The composite reality is, however, more credible somehow, and certainly more unified—like the different styles of the film's two cinematographers—than a similar disjuncture of style would be on stage, unless the boxer-father's character were bracketed as fantastic; or even if we saw it in Brecht, where the disjuncture would be alienated *as* a sign. The almost gratuitous strength of Crisp's performance may be unassimilated even so, as if it were sticking *out* of the film like a thrust of brutalizing fantasy into life.

In theatre, there is an essential disjuncture in performance, the reality of a factitious presence; the form is actualized in proportion to the presence of *that* reality. In Chekov, we are always surprised at how subtle and imperceptible that reality may be, how seemingly natural, though we are also somehow reminded—as at the end of the first act of *The Three Sisters*—that it can only be *as acted*. As the ineffectual festivities of the family romance are dispersed into the ensemble pathos of eroded presence, the nameday party is comically frozen and a photograph is taken, and the acting proceeds as if it were life, with our consciousness that life is acting and acting upon us, more of the Same, interminably, like the baby carriage encircling the stage at the apparent end, with all the repetitive fluency of film which had to be invented for the repetitions. It's as if Chekov had taken the successions of theatre, and its realization, as far as it could go toward life, in the age of photography, before it became cinema.

The theatre's actuality is, however, in the fluent dimensions of the disjuncture between life and theatre, in the *vulnerability* of the acting body, more specifically coterminous with life and more stubbornly resistant to the implication that they are, despite the theatre's own propaganda, one and the same. Whatever the origins of theatre, there is not a memory trace in the form that does not testify to the disturbance caused by life's insistence upon being seen as theatre. That is its subject, and the predicate of its presence, and the theatre has been struggling with that paradox from the beginning—all the more so in that increasingly self-conscious theatre, from Strindberg through Genet and, recently, Robert Wilson, which has also been acquiring the characteristics of film as if that were the answer to the question: Is the whole world a stage or is it not? That's an almost impossible judgment to make, but the theatre is addicted to judgment, about what we can never really be sure is a real question.

The *diegesis* so dear to film semiologists—the obligatory recital of facts in the judicial discourse, all that pertains to the narrative—is an almost obligatory concept in the theatre, which has been judicial, so far as we can tell, through the living memory of the form. We have a record of it in the *Oresteia*—the only extant Greek trilogy—an etiological drama about the nature of justice and the emergence of the jury system from the preoedipal laws of repetitive vengeance. "The law *is* theatre," says Sartre, and the theatre *represents* the law, even in the utmost avoidance of the litigious, as in the theatre forms of the East. If, as appears to be true there, life *is* a dream, what then is theatre? It is the form which—with all the representational means at its disposal, including the power of illusion and the illusory power of its separate presence—resists the truth it is acknowledging in the appearance of what it *is*, which may be impossible to distinguish.

For the struggle in the theatre has always been the struggle with illusion, that obligatory scene, the denial of representation by the representation of the denial—a self-reflexive distrust of its own powers, the fantasy that cancels difference, whether between nature and culture, myth and history, memory and imagination, word and thing, god and man, father and mother, being and becoming, man and woman or—as we "read the meaning in that beacon light" which seems to begin the history of theatre by announcing the end of the war in Troy—reality and illusion, "the interchange of flame and flame":

CHORUS: Yet how can I be certain? Is there some evidence?
CLYTEMNESTRA: There is, there must be; unless a god has lied to me.
CHORUS: Is it dream visions, easy to believe, you credit?
CLYTEMNESTRA: I accept nothing from a brain that is dull with sleep.

Whatever there is in Clytemnestra that causes us to rethink the claims of gender and is still genetically encoded in the theatre, she was not meant to lose it at the movies. That it can be lost in the theatre is apparent from the theoretical writings of Brecht. The Alienation-effect was developed in order to wake up the dozing spectators of the "culinary theatre," where instead of eating popcorn you go to digest your dinner. Brecht, too, expected nothing from a brain that is dull with sleep, and that includes the actor as well as the spectator, from both of whom he wanted critical judgment as the precipitance of not-quite-action but the living capacity *to act.*

What is represented in the theatre, by performance, is the opportunity *for* performance. So far as the spectator is concerned, it may be, as in the classical theatre, performance in a mode of contemplation and figuration. It may appear passive, but there is work to be done, as Marx understood, in reminding us that "The *forming* of the five senses is a labour of the entire history of the world down to the present." In the translating of analogical representation into *effects* of behavior, likeness, identity, and identification, the senses of social man, like those of the actor who is not sleepwalking, are *other* than those of non-social man, though it is this alienated figure who is often thought to be the ideological subject of the movies. When Jean-Louis Comolli wants to reverse that tendency, he speaks of a film of his own in which the theatrical space is reinserted into the cinematic field, so that the viewer and not just the technical apparatus is the operator of the analogical mechanism, desire for the Same reflected "as movement, as trace, mark on faces, gestures, words; in short, theater." Which is critical of the perspective that it constructs. Before theatre becomes theatre, certain intellectual operations have to be performed—though we have seen attempts at forms of theatre which have refused the analogical mechanisms in vain. What we often see in such refusals (as in the participatory anarchy of the sixties) is the pathos of a failed analogy to freedom.

For it makes no difference if the performance leaves the stage. That is no less ideological than before, and naively ideological to boot, for what it amounts to is a self-deluding shift in the order of representation. What we encounter is the non-theatrical illusion, a theatricality exposed to the illusions of its own demystifications. As the duplications of realism destroy the appearance of a repetition of reality by the impurity of signalling differences, so any performance splits off from itself the analogizing propensity of the very idea of performance. As for realistic drama, there the most immaculate effects of representation, as we see in Chekov, most fully belie the representation, certifying the image *as* image, with all the combinatorial play upon the illusion of reality and the reality of illusion that keeps the image in its place as image; that is, the thing by means of which we are deceived. One must be deceived by the image in order to *see* the image. Were we to see what it is representing we wouldn't believe it for an instant, I mean the image—for the other we never see, though the desire to do so never ceases. "You must pierce the wall," writes Kafka. "Piercing it is not difficult; it is made of paper. What is difficult is not to be deceived by the fact that there is already a painting on paper representing the way you pierce the wall, so exceedingly deceptive that you are tempted to say, 'Don't I pierce it continually?' "

What the theatre does, then, is to bring into presence what, without theatre, cannot be present—not unlike, in the psychoanalytical process, the making-present-in-consciousness what seems past or out of memory, the presentness depending, however, on its becoming *consciously* past for the first time. So, this thing which appears, and appears *because* remembered, never was before the remembrance, which composes it, a real illusion, factitiously rehearsed, like the delusion-formation of Freud's Schreber, which was an attempt at reconstitution or recovery of the past, something other than a delusion to the extent that, in its rehearsal, it was being-formed. The theatre event, even when not realistic, is a testing of reality in a formative process, by making it up as it goes along, another thing. Neither the reality being tested nor the reality composed exist outside the activity of performance, which is not to deny that there is still another reality objectively there, external to the consciousness being performed. The re-sources of credibility are drawn both from the process and that to which, insensibly, the process is being referred through the senses, with their authorizing credentials. What is being rehearsed into performance is *a series of choices.* Which is why the issue of responsibility is there, in the play, as it can never be on film, where all the choices have been made and, re-viewed, are inevitably afterthought. That is why we can expect the cinema, with its impression of reality, to sustain what Metz calls its basic bond with the theatre, where thought is basic because fleshed out. The theatre is too corporeally real to be thought real, but it is *really thought*, the senses having become in practice, as Marx says in an early text, "direct theoreticians." So, too, the eye becomes a human eye, "when its object has become a social, human object produced by man and destined for him." It can only be destined for him if he's awake.

If the theatre has a legacy of the judicial, it is generically theoretical. The word theatre comes from the same Greek roots as theory, having to do with watching and the place of watching, the two meeting in *speculation*—an idea much explored in film theory, but without much emphasis on the corollary: that it implies a kind of *vigilance* as well, as with The Watchman who awakens from a fabulous preoedipal dark to open the *Oresteia*, as if what will be seen has already been seen, through the long duration of observant thought: "I speak to those who understand, but if they fail, I have forgotten everything." The Watchman speaks, too, with the observed solitariness of occulted caution, as to the initiates of a Mystery, for it's a mystery that he wants us to understand. There's something about the occultation that makes us see it, something intrinsic to the nature of the theatre, which is not merely play but catechistic play, the play of thought and the thought of play, mnemonic and demonic—a kind of animated brain fever with a metaphysical obsession, approaching Panic, the god who may have lied. The theatre has reason for being nervous, for there's emperiled mortality in its power. In the theatre it is not only that the line between presence and absence is blurred, but the line between presence and panic—which is to say that the ontological condition of stage fright is borne into performance and, with no editing out, remains an active if subliminal component of what we see. Sometimes the actor is so anxious we can hardly see, as if the anxiety were the Mystery, and it possibly is.

Every now and then—through years of watching in the dark—you wonder what keeps a performance from breaking down. We tend to think of actors as exhibitionistic, but I've also felt that the first thing an actor wants to do when he gets on stage is to get off as fast as he can. *What keeps him there?* The motives are figured in traditional drama by the interdependent tropes of Will, Necessity, and Chance—although the drama is always asking, as the actor does in his craft, where does one begin and the other end? Sometimes, whatever it is that we call presence seems—as Lévi-Strauss says of the enigma of the prohibition of incest—the answer to which there is no question. Isn't that the significance of the second, more enigmatic appearance of the Ghost, in the Closet, where the previously *embodied* Ghost, visibly acted, is not-there; not as in the voided space of film, but literally so?

To the degree that film is a more direct representation of the unconscious than theatre, it confirms what Freud wrote in his essay on "The Uncanny," that "our unconscious has as little use now as ever for the idea of its own mortality"—which is not exactly true of the Ghost, with its almost unimaginable effort of rematerializing will and the poignant memory of its once-smooth body, scarred now like the walls of time, where all the moral imperatives are blurred. The most compelling presence in the theatre is, any way you look at it, perishable goods, vulnerable, trying desperately not to believe it, nothing you can depend on, nothing will come of nothing, much ado about nothing, nothing to be done, never, never, never, never, never. Where, at the limits of theatre, in the dialectics of negation—unduplicatable but driven to repetition—some self-cancelling avatar of desire, sonorous and immaterial, seems almost to pass onto film. There are exquisite moments of theatre where this is especially so, where anyone who has ever directed has wished he could get it on camera, and then unwishes it if it is to remain wholly theatre, realized in its vanishings, as in the final moments of *Lear*, where the intimacy of absence is such it can hardly be looked at, but perhaps seen only with the unaided eye: "Look on her! Look her lips,/ Look there, look there—" On the other side of the avalanche, more of the Same.

It's at these vanishing moments that we feel most tellingly the temporal inflexion of the actor's vulnerability—the more so the more realized *by* the actor—and the particular vulnerability of the theatre itself, possessed with disappearance, the differences that *must* be seen, like the differences between forms at their limits.

In cinema, the analogue of the actor's mortality is the deterioration of the film, which starts at its inception, and therefore becomes the paradigm of a disappearing presence, despite the notion of a *printed* text, fixed by chemicals—these ideas becoming the coordinates by which we play the game of its absence. There is also the issue of how well the printing is done and how well the film is screened, the condition of the screen itself (I saw one recently with a stain through the projection like a glyph of Clyfford Still) and the condition of that particular filmstrip, although practical reason tells us there is some sort of real difference between a person who *is* dying and a film that can be replaced, another copy struck, perhaps not an exact clone, but better than we are likely to have with human beings for a while. So as regards the power of a disappearing presence, the theatre would appear to have the advantage, its very corporeality being the basis of its most powerful illusion, that something is substantially there, the thing itself, even as it vanishes. There are many apparent causes of stage fright, but that may be the final ground. Presence in acting is something more than charisma or the energy that makes us say the actor is all there. (Sometimes he is, but he isn't very much.) What *is* there, however, is the dimensionality of time through the actor, ether of time. Of all the performing arts, the theatre stinks most of mortality. If the theatre is perverse or corrupt, it is because it is also time-serving in this sense.

I'm not sure that we're conscious in the cinema as we are in the theatre of the discrepancy between the interval of time as performed and the duration of life as lived. We speak of the two- or three-hour traffic of the stage, but we're unlikely to think of film in such measure because of the versatile negotiability of cinematic time: arrest, reversal, speedup, and various kinds of optical exchange, the synthetic time-warp of montage, splicing, segmenting, so that we almost want to see the spaces between frames, a virtual suspension of time, in the intoxicating control of succession, the feeling that time, after all, is possessed by the cinematic machine, the primal illusion of the moving strip, the wished benediction of its beginnings. This is not the exactitude of dimensioned time of classical practice in the theatre, where the compression of time, and the famous Unity, is a proposition about life, and the relationship of life and art in another order of reality. As experienced in the movies, time exists (as the theatre has so well stated the other proposition:) between a sleep and a forgetting—either technically, producing an image in the frequency of frames, or reminding us that time is without dimension, the merest illusion of an extension, in the redolence of those absent objects or the patina of our gaze; in the stricture of speculation through our fictions of space.

In the theatre, where space is *designated* (even if disrupted), we are much more conscious, I think, of the overlay of playing time upon lifetime, and the painful inadequacy to it, an epistemological foreshortening that is also, in tragedy, an admission of defeat. If there is the residue of old ritual it is in this compression of apparently discrete events which seem to remember in the play within the play an older infinity of play that existed before time. Even when it is performed in the open air, as in the infancy of the form, the theatre always has a sense of belatedness, and not immediacy, to it—as if it were born with impacted memory. It is this born-again redundancy in the *memento mori*, not merely the circling of the immediate upon the real that can be incessantly projected, that accounts for the peculiar strangeness of the theatre, which is not to any degree like film a product of the world's affluence and which doesn't seem to remember unless it *pretends* to forget, though it has forgotten nothing, or there would be no play.

There has been in recent experimental theatre a lot of sentimental longing for myth and ritual, a romance with instant archetypes; but even when the theatre was still closely affiliated with ritual, it knew that it was just pretending, and what we have in performance is not so much a ritual event as the ghost of a ritual pretense. The theatre is a far more skeptical form than film, by nature, whatever else is imposed upon it—film having emerged in consonance with the novel out of the fictive aspirations of the legacy of romance. In theatre, the body's specific gravity is always there, subject to time, astride of a grave. About the older infinity of play before time: that is almost congenitally distrusted in the form. The self-reflexive play within the play is an obsessive mechanism of the theatre, like the mechanisms of paranoia, but unlike the current discourse on film (with its admixture of literary and feminist theory), the theatre is never content with the theoretical prospect of a field of endless play. Whatever it contributes, in theory, to the textual dispersal of all forms, the theatre remembers the unstateable undercurrent of play which inevitably makes the actor sweat.

Play is dreadful. It is the mere passage of unthinking time, thinking making it so, as we saw in Gogo's fist which, for the moment, wanted to put an end to play. As for those minutiae that Ibsen wanted to preserve, sometimes so etiolated as to seem out of sight, there may be, as I said before, a momentary instinct for wanting them on film, but the persuasive intuition of their presence *is* their evanescence, a living indeterminacy that can never be studied again, *that way*—because, in a very strict sense, it is the actor's mortality which is the acted subject, for he is right there dying in front of your eyes. The critical thing, then, in the institution of theatre is not so much that an actor is there, but that an actor is so vulnerably there. Whatever he represents in the play, in the order of time he is representing nobody but himself. How could he? that's his body, doing time.

The cinematic institution, like the film festival which is a part of it, shifts the locus of vulnerability from the film, the art-object, or the actors in the film (if there are actors)—the image of human agency in the narrative—to its *representatives*. I won't use another term because, theoretically, the textualization of film, as with the book, has made the author-creator disappear as it has made the subject "problematical." This is all the more ironically so as the assault on representation continues. Thus, there may be a lot of badmouthing at a festival, or even a riot, but the film by then, unless scissored in projection or symbolically heisted, is safe in the can while certain people are being abused. The actors in the film may not even be present, or if the director is he is part of the discourse. As for the the film, even if it is destroyed, there are other copies. In the theatre, however, the question of the subject and the ambiguities of presence disappear—at least for the moment—when the actor is assaulted or arrested or, as I have seen it, the show is stopped by blacks, feminists, or—not to suggest parity of purpose—lunatics who are apolitical, but who (with a logic more or less justified by the schizoanalysis of the *Anti-Oedipus*) might, as has been done in the past, leap upon the stage and attack Iago for his dirty seeming.
When that happens, it's not the transcendental subject or the absent presence which is in danger, but the otherwise missing person, the one who breathes and eats and shits and fucks, *homo ludens* as *homo historia*, who may have to decide right there, diachronically, whether he means it or is merely pretending. I mean is he willing to stand by what he represents, like the "unperfect actor on the stage" in Shakespeare's sonnet, "Who with his fear is put beside his part"? A film doesn't blush when it has to go out and perform the night after bad reviews. Nor does it have to summon up—as actors in my own work have done—the will to play against severe hostility, that presence which enters an actor's performance in sometimes crushing, sometimes dialectical collaboration with the subliminal residues of stage fright. *Cruising* just played at our local cinema, and the gays protested. But Al Pacino, who suffered through his embarrassment *in* the film (the embarrassment registered as indelibly as his permanent wave) is no doubt involved by now in another project and can keep a secure distance from the filmic event—unless, like Vanessa Redgrave, he chooses to make of a given showing the semblance of a confrontational appearance which,

if sufficiently publicized, will change the way we see the film, but not a mini-frame of her performance.

Theatre is not an Action but a pre-tense of action, an adumbration or incipience, the annunciation of an infinitive which the cinema cuts off. So far as the problem of identity is concerned, the whole body vociferates. Even in the silence of mime, the theatre is *giving voice*. It is not only that we suffer an anxious empathy when the actor forgets his lines, but when the actor gets really anxious, the first thing to go is the voice. In film, it can be doctored on the soundtrack or recorded another time. On stage, the loss of voice is the worst of all inflictions, the contingency that really hurts, bringing us painfully back to life, the watchers and the watched. Theatre becomes more like film, in another sense, when the actor's vulnerability is at a minimum, when it virtually becomes for all its dialogue a silent partner to the absence, time-serving in the cruder sense (the dialogue being, in our conventional theatre, a coverup for the silence), entering the structure of the discourse determined by the entropic agencies of power, the media, and most profoundly fantasized, and perpetuated, by the politics of discourse of film and, despite its demystification of the apparatus of cinematic power, the extension of that discourse in theory—what Metz calls the theodicy of indulgence.

Before I conclude with more of that, let me observe that there are, in our established theatres, plays whose surface is very little different, whose articulation in performance is so mechanically perfect, and yet so vacuous, they might as well be film—which is not saying a film version of the same *is* the same, just more of it, the enervating libidinal tithe from the same psychic fount, the same repressive apparatus in the overall system of production and consumption, and counting on the same capacity (not necessity) for submissiveness in the viewer. There are more of them in the cinema but they come from the same ideological story board. When, in the theatre, we wonder where the audiences have gone, they have gone where there's more of it, more of the Same, what we increasingly find coming on stage from the ideological dispensation of film, as if the two forms were a continuum, as I think they are, with a break in the bonding like one of those bone fractures in the oedipal clubfoot that don't even show up in the x-ray.

Critical theory is presumably charged with making such distinctions, with seeing what cannot quite be seen, but one of the things I've meant by more of the Same is the presence of theory in the fantasies of power—though in the American theatre we may have to talk of its absence, because as compared to film there is next to no theory at all. This is especially true about the speculative presence of the audience, whose Authority is still cynically sanctified as the Last Judgment by those who would manipulate it as if it were brainless and had no judgment at all. Which is more often true than not, as it is more epidemically in the movies, where it is often given theoretical ground.

Nothing I've ever written has aroused such animosity among the cynical as the statement (years ago) which seems an understatement now: Give an audience a chance, it will inevitably be wrong. But that assumes, through all the fantasies of replicating desire, in the infinite deferrability of meaning, that we still believe judgments can be made. Worse, that judgments need to be made. I say this in an atmosphere of harsh judgment by those who, in the new doxology of deconstruction, legislate the open-ended, the ceaselessly mutating eroticism of postponement, polymorphous and parodic, a "pure jubilatory discourse," coming attractions, in the siren voice of *jouissance*. If it were more like that, as it is in much of Barthes, I might continue to forgo judgment, but is it not true that one often hears the invocation of a receptive and feminine space in a voice which insists (through a formidable jargon) that the play of interpretation is absolutely privileged, and that's the only conclusion you can come to.

Sometimes the heavy arsenal of film theory reminds me of *The Great Dictator*, when Chaplin yanks a cord on Big Bertha and the shell plops out of the phallocentrism like a gum-drop orgasm, and the Barber, sent to defuse it, finds it alarmingly activated in his wary orbit, feeble as it is, real, and dangerous, and no kidding—parody never sufficient to power. Or the scene in which he and Reginald Gardiner are upside down in the byplane with the dispatch case, containing the hermeneutic cipher that will save the day; thinking they are right side up, the Barber also trying to keep time in place as his watch rises in space, by pushing down on its signifying chain, amnesia following the crash as the Barber emerges from a Black Hole or cloaca or the preoedipal maternal slime into the contingencies of the Reality Principle. Or the sequence in *Modern Times* where the head of the foreman is locked, as in a guillotine, upside down in the huge flywheels and gears of a sort of desiring machine, and Chaplin sticks a stalk of celery in his mouth so that the discourse is returned for a moment to the vegetal silence of plenitude.

Or—when I think of the political fantasies of the theoretical discourse—the dictator Hynkel doing his ballet with the balloon of world power, not only power punctured for the fools who have it, but the fantasies of non-aggressive power for the fools who don't. Or, at the end of *Modern Times*, the seductive exhortation of the final smile of Goddard by the Tramp, an artifice of radiance, a construction, summoning up its possibility by pure fiction, nothing to go on but a wish, dispelling what Derrida names "the *dead time* within the presence of the living present, within the general form of all presence"—as they disappear up the road, shuffle and virginal buttocks, divided by the white line of impeding difference, returning to mountains and horizon, also down the Originary Trace, putting the dead time to work when jobs remain scarce or have lost their savor. Or the writing flying off the Tramp's wrist before—in an aboriginal babble of polyglottal words—"shifting the signified a great distance," and "throwing, so to speak, the anonymous body of the actor into [the] ear: it granulates, it crackles, it caresses, it grates, it cuts, it comes":—but then it *goes*, that bliss, because it never forgets, in the joyous presence of the disjunct soundtrack, that the shifted distance is only about as long as the watch's chain; and that if neutered pleasure, its "force of *suspension*" of a centered system or philosophy of meaning "can never be overstated," as Barthes declares, the force of that system can never be overstated either, like the strength of the proscenium when Gogo struck, the *jouissance* of power laughing up its abesnt sleeve.

What strikes me about these Chaplinesque reflections on the activity of theory is that, as theory, they are very discrete about the limiting condition of pure presence. When we feel, as Barthes did, "a certain need to *loosen* the theory a bit," lest the ideolect repeat itself, Chaplin reminds us that there is in every libidinal flow theoretical trace-lines circumscribing the Imaginary, the Symbolic and the Real, but keeping, through the impeccable eloquence of seeming innocence, an unstinting eye on those other lines, prison lines, soup lines, goose-stepping lines of pure force, and other eternal lines to time which are, whatever the hidden agendas of the Lacanian mirror phase, written clearly enough: "TEN DAYS LATER." The blank and darkened screen with those plain words in quotes tells more than a narrative story, and the duration of its projection is not only relatively, immeasurably, meant for reading or opened to desire, but—as in the interludic inscriptions of a Brecht play, as after the Great Capitulation of Mother Courage—also meant to return us, libido abated and in the simpler sense, to political and social reality, outside of the rectifying fantasies of metonymic and playful words, or the orthographic reifications of cinematic bliss.

Flights of Angels, Scattered Seeds

●

I AM NOT AN ORTHODOX JEW, NOR EVEN VERY MUCH REFORMED, SINCE there was never any clear reverence to fall away from. If not by doctrine, then by some instinct of divided mind I recall—as I think about where the theatre will be fifteen, or fifty, years from now—Walter Benjamin's remark that "the Jews were prohibited from investigating the future." They are, however, instructed in *remembrance*, which strips the future of its magic. Perhaps the future has been prematurely given a bad name, stripped too caustically of its magic by certain prophetic Jews—if not the chiliastic Marx, the discontented Freud— although it is in the tradition of the prophets to understand that a look into the future is a remembrance of things to come, in the belabored nightmare from which we are trying to awaken, a salvaging of the spilled seeds of time, putting the best complexion on the forbidden.

What I want to do here, more or less at random (and maybe in the sere), is to pick up some of the seeds, as a reflex of speculation—not unlike the theatrework I've tried to do over the last dozen years which, so far as I can see, still remains to be done. In the *thought* of such a theatre the subject *is* the future, but with a particular consciousness about the *remainder, in* the doing *as* it's done, doing it over and over. It is a theatre of *reflexions* with the actor in the space between predication and prediction, without resolving the difference between them, but entrusting it to the moment, as if the subject were the self. We've become accustomed in our time to structures of momentary thought, associative or additive, going over the same ground, serially, but aside from the (un)grounding, no promise that anything will add up. How?

By what measure? and *who* would know? for isn't that the sticking point, the summary other (*what* audience?) of the recurring subject? in which thought becomes a *process* with no other evidence but itself? the Geiger counter in the Lacanian mirror? It is a silverless mirror with indeterminate frames whose outside danger is solipsism. With the solipsist, as in outer space, time warps into the future catching us from behind, disturbing the circadian rhythms, and the problem is where we came from, assuming we know where we are.

These are all questions *in* the future of the theatre, which may be read in the scattered seeds, and *represented* in the theatre of the future. The imminence of another orthodoxy is already in the scattering, and it's hard to imagine theatre activity of any importance that does not accept it as something like second nature, to which, naturally, there may develop an internal resistance, as there is in what I say. In the habit of the modern, the emphasis is on process, but refusing to take for granted the perpetual present moment in which the future is *only* the subject, self-perceived, almost wholly a specular fiction; which is to say, *theatre*, the sum of moments to be watched; which has been almost wantonly appropriated by not only the other arts but the most seductive critical theory, as it tries to assume the character of a performance.

It should already be apparent that this is very circuitous thought, divided about the subject, but to the extent we are talking about theatre we are talking about *division*, here and now, now and then, body and thought, in the engendering of the subject, sex and substance, self and other (which in the mirror is infinitely divided), the future and its object—which, by narrowing the distance between art and life, may be a better theatre, but is always life and death. If the theatre has any future, it is in wanting to do away with it, the future, theatre, and division, for that has always been *its* subject, the millenial desire, the "future in the instant," the undivided subject, in an incessancy of becoming act and being One, with the moment as its medium taking us where it will. We used to think of it as Faustian, but it's really the same subject even if laid back, chewing upon the seeds.

We can also pretend, of course, that the seeds are no longer there, only the scattering, like a memory trace on the mystic writing pad, which Freud used to explain the perceptual apparatus of the mind and the discontinuity in the currents of innervation from the unconscious, which may be "at the bottom of the origin of the concept of time." But as I think about the possibility, seeding the possibility, I do so with equivocal feelings about affiliated tendencies, in thought and performance: the addiction to process itself, the aleatory, the evasive habitudes of chance, disjuncture and condensation, and the encyclicals of seriality which would otherwise, in the performance of thought, authorize a more elliptical procedure.

i

Say, rather, we are following in the wake (I wanted to say dialectically, but let it pass) of Benjamin's angel of history, drawn from Klee's *Angelus Novus*, moving away from something which, in the picture, he is "fixedly contemplating." As Benjamin reads the image, his/its "face is turned to the past." Fifteen years? fifty years? (assuming we endure them), likely to make no essential difference whatever the apparencies of change, because of the sovereignty of chance refusing the essential, as if the ancient forms of theatre in their incarnadizing myths had accurately recorded history in advance. This angel is no fuzzy archetype from the *illud tempus* or occult fancy from the *Anima Mundi*. He is moving *in* history. Or *with* history. Yet the more we study the gaze the less sure we are in what direction he is moving, or whether he is or we are, the geography of the temporal being confounded: "Where we perceive a chain of events, he sees one single catastrophe which keeps piling wreckage upon wreckage and hurls it in front of his feet. The angel would like to stay, awaken the dead, and make whole what has been smashed. But a storm is blowing from Paradise; it has got caught in his wings with such violence that the angel can no longer close them. This storm irresistibly propels him into the future to which his back is turned, while the pile of debris before him grows skyward. This storm is what we call progress."

ii

In a period which seems to be advancing scandalously to its ruin, progress also has a bad name. So long already, it smells to high heaven. But not (as I write) at Madison Square Garden where, during the Democratic Convention, the word is being used so liberally and with such unexpected sincerity—by Ted Kennedy or by Muriel Humphrey before the testimonial film about Hubert—that it is almost touching, like a lapse of history. Or the effect of photography itself, and film, with its power to elicit sentiments that are moving, memorial and—even when not merely documentary, in the most admirable state of the art—maybe meretricious, because of its insidious manipulations of time. The threat of the photograph was absorbed into the theatre in the foreground of *The Wild Duck*, as if to keep it away from time. But as with other perplexities of our age, we are now dealing with *quantity*, the exponential powers of swifter production, the inestimable forces of distribution, and the rabid critical publicity about the quality of photographic art.

iii

The qualities of photography which are saturating the image-system—annotating history with a non-existent code—are not to be discounted in the future of the theatre, another reproductive system, saturated with time, whose credibility has been so undermined by the analogical plenitude of the other that it has sometimes tried to behave, in recent years, as if it *weren't* theatre. Or, in order to be more convincing, has had to insist that more *work*—that is, productive labor—go into the *making* of its images, the construction exposed, whereas in older realistic acting we didn't want the work to show, as in the cinema, where what is exposed is not the construction but, as they say, the visible presence of the invisible. No wonder we've seen a generation of actors who, in their psychophysical exercises, have learned to sweat. There is also a sweat which comes with the invisible, as when you see a ghost, and the body may be drenched with both, but with no way to work it off. It was a new labor force which was uncertain about the future from the beginning, nurtured through catastrophe in a cloud of unknowing, the wreckage in its memory like a strip of film, no longer sure what images are supportable—nor where, with any scale, they might be performed if they were made. That's what we saw at the end of the sixties—after, at Chicago, they chanted, "The whole world is watching!" and maybe it was, for the moment—in the breakdown of body language, and the sweat became a strain without the amplitude of history.

iv

The alternative seems to be a public solitude (Stanislavski) without a public. Still: vigilant as we may be about what the course of history represents—about the history of representation itself, with its illusions, one of which is progress—it's hard to think about the future at all without the illusion of progress sneaking in, if only as an isotope of relief over survival, as if the mere fact that we've made it so far is an improvement. Or as if the different things that happen are the things which really should, the capacity for distinction blurring in the sheer abundance, as with photography—or solo and private performances (an alternative to unemployment, as well as repression)—so that we don't know whether we're getting on with it or disappearing into the profusion.

v

On the wincing anvil of a premonition: There is a pulsation of something like this, a progressive vanishing? or a vanishing progress?, in the *"fixed gaze"* of Beckett's Clov (who wants to be a solo performer, outside of history), resembling the Angelus Novus, something taking its course that he can't quite keep out, the long trail of repeatable catastrophe, two thousand years of western history like a propagating stalemate in his voice: "Finished, it's finished, nearly finished, it must be nearly finished. (*Pause.*) Grain upon grain, one by one, and one day, there's a heap, a little heap." We might very well have been discouraged, but the heap is fabulous. I am not exaggerating, I am being very discrete. There is an anti-entropic nominalist signal (*Watt:* "No symbol where none intended") in the permutating stasis, with its simulacra of motion exquisitely denying change, or rather change denying motion. The heap is not quite the Smithsonian sublimity of the *Spiral Jetty* or *Amarillo Ramp*, but it is moving subliminally in a similar whorled and oxymoronic direction.

vi

Once, at some threatening impasse of a rehearsal for a theatrework we were doing, extruded from *Hamlet*, I asked the actors: if you could change anything in the universe of Elsinore (the eventual name of the work, its metaphysical ground), what would you change? The afflatus of the question was intended to ward off the high energy of an enveloping pessimism in a surfeit of play, the familiar cloacal tug of the nihilism of the modern, our classic heritage—encouraged by certain self-reflexive abrasions in the nature of our work. The question was a somewhat hedging version of Brecht's insistence, out of the early nihilism of his work, that however complete reality may seem it has to be transformed by art so that it can be seen as changeable and acted upon as such. At ground zero, where ideology is next to nothing—and that's where we felt we were—we wanted *as a last resort* to distinguish *non*-meanings from *no*-meanings. In our own acting through the alternatives—in an effort to mend the lesion between action and reflection—the options were narrowing down to the last pinched nerve of thought. Could we wince out another value?

vii

It was something like what must have happened in the evolution of Arabic numerals when—in the disturbing process of taking things away from each other—they came upon the concept of zero, lifting the round figure at the end of a row of digits and giving it another use. The importance of that idea was recognized by the Arabs in one of the most incisive remarks in the history of mathematics: "When nothing is left over, then write the little circle so that the place does not remain empty." That they had something against emptiness may be a bit of good fortune. Could the zero itself be the vatic inscription of a possible meaning? That is, I suppose, what one finally means by taking nothing for granted. That nothing is, through the determining negation of the cosmos, not only the source of play but the incursive symbol of a revolving chance, the wheel of fortune—like the pirate ship circling in a zone of indifference and, to keep the Plot going, bringing Hamlet back.

viii

There is a sign in such a return, improbable as it is. It is the tentative disclosure of another possibility in what is *already there* . . .

ix

"Rediscovered miraculously after what absence in perfect voids it is no longer quite the same," as Beckett says in *Imagination Dead Imagine*, "from this point of view, but there is no other"—though there are various structures of performance which have been trying to make another value out of (not accident but) the *recurrency* of accident, the displaced circle circling upon itself in a widening orbit of old names (time space matter mind), moving from zero towards infinity in an accelerating leap (in the microcosm as in the macrocosm), like the stochastic processes of a static universe where the "red shifts" and Doppler effects of quasi-stellar sources seem to arise from the high velocities of *recession* (in the line of sight) of the galaxies, so that no matter where we look the galaxies are running away from us, and no matter where we are situated the picture would be the same, though recent observations seem to indicate that the radio sources *increase* in number (through the static) the more that space gathers itself backwards (into time).

x

The instellar dimensions seem larger but we are back with Zeno's arrow and his noisy bushel of corn, grain upon grain, the Ent which is the Non-Ent which is not, the paradoxes of predication reverberating, the trajectory of the tortoise moving with the speed of light—as in the stunning attenuations of Wilson's operas where the future, aphasic, momentarily lost, whirls upon itself, like the cybernetic redundancy (of information theory) which is necessary to get through the "noise."

xi

And if the body resists the predication, the paradox spurs on the brain. The brain has a lot of moves. Thought is nimble. "If the dull substance of my flesh were thought," says the Lover in the sonnet longing for the Loved One, "Injurious distance should not stop my way. . . ." As Shakespeare and Beckett remember, Ceres, goddess of grain, is phonemically embraced by the cerebral. (Which is not quite Concept Art.) "Look! There! All that rising corn!" But the liability of the whirling paradox is that it scatters into parody. In the afterimage of thought thought will not be fooled. Parody is a coverup, as nobody knows better than Hamm. An explosion in the bushel: "(*Pause. Violently.*) Use your head, can't you, use your head, you're on earth, there's no cure for that."

xii

The difference between that outburst of Hamm—who wants to be a *whole* actor, playing all the roles—and most "conceptual" performances is that the latter have lost the high humanistic velocity of the seemingly static desire travelling over vast spaces of thought, which invented the *idea* of a future that, relinquished too much to the *moment,* we're now struggling to preserve by discontinuous structures which draw it out. The next fifteen years are likely to be, not always with Wilson's brilliance, a disjunct holding action.

xiii

When, in the shift from the sovereignty of pleasure-pain to the Reality Principle, *thought* appears in the *mise en scène* of the unconscious as a "restraint of motor discharge (of action)," Freud describes it (in his 1911 essay on "Two Principles of Mental Functioning") as " essentially an experimental way of acting. . . . For this purpose conversion of free cathexis into 'bound' cathexes was imperative, and this was brought about by means of raising the level of the whole cathectic process."

xiv

Once they called it Destiny and now we call it Structure. I don't mean they are the Same. For the kind of experiment we have at any time depends upon the degree and quality of *resistance* to the moment, even when you think you're letting it be, and a sense of its *duration*, which determines the features we attribute to time, a river a rosebud a sediment or a dream, a sparrow through the meadhall or a falling star, a figure with a wallet at its back or a blank check for a linguistic event, the kneejerk interval of a conception or a limitless metonymic space where, as a dance or a play of light or other impulses of behavior by human bodies or other objects, the A-series is reducible to the B-series since A-determinations can be performed in terms of B-relations between events, or vice versa . . .

xv

Today we live, it seems, in a dispensation of moments or infinite profusion of instants which the weakening human presence of theatre can barely endure, yet with an avidity for the instants that we want to see imaged, out of some obsessional hunger for figuration that nobody understands. The demand is insatiate, as if we were suffering in a colloidal suspension of images from sensory deprivation. We call for a Theatre of Images to keep up with the proliferations that not even the flashing and clicking ubiquity of photography can appease. For there is something about its still-enshrouded photochemical processes piling up memories for the future like a loss of memory, which is the wrong kind of remembrance—the anecdotal accumulations of an information system storing up alms for oblivion, as if in dread of being forgotten. All those images, unregenerately *out of touch*. A double dream of *nature morte*, like the achievement of duration without desire.

xvi

That is not the duration of theatre. But if all the world's becoming the stage which was once a metaphor of the world, most of it is now on film, while the metaphor clings to the theatre, with its bodily mortgage of time. What we once saw in the forms on stage (like John Ashbery in Parmigianino in his own convex mirror) was a certain measure of ideality, there because we saw it, dreaming *what* we saw—until an emptiness is tangibly there whose meaning we cannot see, though we can't deny it *is* there—not the meaning but the tangibility. Whatever it is we see is nourished by the dream of seeing, which is the reversed image of a desire to *be-seen*, which—in the gluttony of our scopic drive—is almost being exhausted on film.

xvii

Louis Lumière, whose claw-drive for the filmstrip gave the projective impetus to cinema, said about his own invention, "The cinematograph is an invention without a future." Historians of the cinema have condescended to the remark, which seems so naively far from the dominant reality of the cinematic apparatus, but it remains to be seen who has the last laugh. For it may be that the cinematograph has indeed come full circle, like most mechanical inventions, to the end of its progress—unless it once again comes to terms with theatre. We can already see that occurring in film theory, which scorned it after Bazin. We can also see it in the performative clues of the most abstract films (without open evidence of dramatic narrative, or actors). The enigmatic traces give the invisibility away by leaving, say, sprocket marks or a lock of hair upon the film, like that left by the filial stranger upon Agamemnon's tomb. After years of insistence upon the autonomy of film the antioedipal discourse of cinema seems not to be able to rid itself of theatre, whose death appears now as its most demonic illusion, or something like an interminable disease.

xviii

I am speaking of the theatre in which (the oedipal) *filiation* is still the issue, and the enigma, the disease or villainy of which the drama has said much and I shall want to say more. The theatre of the future will certainly be affected by the labyrinthine outreach of the cinematic apparatus, as it has been in the no-win competition for audiences. It will also respond to whatever technology surrounds it, which may even change our ideas as to what constitutes an audience. The point is that we must conceive of technology now as something other than machines. The stress in social thought is on systems of communication, with mechanisms of production and distribution in the unconscious, a technology which is mirroring "epistemic codes" or the performance of "desiring-machines."

xix

In these processes, the industrialization of imagery by the movies, and by video, may be the controlling force, since there is a technological obsession with *recurrency*, the looping concatenation of fragments (splicing, cutting, superimpositions), a new allegorical neurosis of recycling, feedback, biodegradability ("loop gains" and "return ratios" mimicking, efferently, the proprioceptive signals of the body and the central regulatory programs of the species), a whole new repertoire of replicative strategies which will have to be reassessed (is being reassessed) by social theorists, because they are, ironically, strategies of *accumulation*, like a shadow-play of the old disreputable system—the computer terminals disconnected before they are installed in every home because the metaphor of an uninterrupted series, the dream of repetitive sequences of ceaseless differences and timeless moments, the systematic disjunctures of a spatiotemporal experience with no apparent organic limit of magnitude has turned out to be (like the "geometric grammaticality" of Sol LeWitt's cities of cubes and the ontological hysteria of Richard Foreman) a systemic variant of uninterrupted illusion, like the society of overabundance and no-scarcity which preceded it and encountered, in the syntagmatic chain of events, a broken-down economy, stagflation, and the paratactically rising expectations of OPEC, whose member countries not only have the oil but an organic corner, to end this period, on the tradition of the arabesque.

xx

We used to believe that theatre reflects society. If it remains to any extent a public form, holding the (split) mirror up to nature, then we will expect experiment in the theatre to keep pace somehow, in whatever subterranean ways, with the more activist projections of a post-industrial world. Theory and fantasy conspire in a promise of recombinant wonders through the displacement of labor into information, instantly transmitted by satellite, the terminals at every elbow, in a cybernetic transfer of the dematerialized body of thought. As for the body itself, there is the incalculable cracking of the genetic code, and a new genesis by implantation. We are asked, as with abortion, to think through the right-to-life as we haven't really done since the reported death of tragedy. These will also be space laboratories which can achieve in surgery, at zero gravity, another fusion of fragments impossible on earth, medical miracles of levitation, a transcendent healing of the dismembered body, as if there we'll finally have the shamanism at which the theatre has been pretending, with the dull substance of its flesh, shoes left at the door, its unfortunate feet on the ground. (Mircea Eliade, by the way, disturbed by the percussive presumptions, called it "family shamanism.")

xxi

When we imagine theatre on other planets, we are not really imagining a future (no less with extraterrestrial intelligence) but indemnifying the past, whose "secret heliotropism" is always at work—as Benjamin says in a Blakean image—like the flower turning itself to the sun, in the unenvying present, which doesn't *want* a future, only itself.

xxii

Thus, coming back to earth, like Gravity's Rainbow:

xxiii

The actuality is, for the time being, not what the future-planners are predicting. Not yet, not probably for the fifty years limit of our ruminations. What we are more likely to see is another holding action, the revitalization of heavy industry which, through a long period of overweening consumption and improvident under-investment, left us holding the bag from which, in the Energy Crisis, the seeds were running out. The theatre had been predicting that crisis with almost hysterical energy through the history of modernism, as Woyzeck's running razor, like Occam's gone berserk, widened into Wedekind's Jack the Ripper, and the tower that Solness built had, in the hallucinations of Strindberg, a crack in the chimney before the oneiric remembrance of the petrifying fall—and what else are we talking about in the amortizing paralytics of Beckett, the bag in the mud of *Comment c'est?*, which is why I have been returning to him as the *locus classicus* of the problematic of the future.

xxiv

With a more direct experience of the scattering on impact, after the Blitz and the Bomb, Germany and Japan had the almost ontological advantage of beginning over again, building fuel-efficient factories along with higher-mileage cars and, now with a cultural gift for miniaturization, Japan apparently has better superconductors for the cybernetic universe when it finally establishes its dominion. Over the forseeable future, and despite the necessity for going solar or nuclear or both, we are still likely to be digging for coal—and in a world of images, that image is still germane to the future of the theatre, with the rumor of its long ascent from the underground and, like Freud, like Kafka, its history of excavations. *Comment c'est?* Whether beginning or ending (and picking up the pun:), it seems to be in language or, as they say semiotically, in the language-systems. In the postmortems of the anti-verbal sixties (which are also being recycled in critical theory), we have had some strip mining—as in the language-games of Minimalism and Conceptual Art—but insufficient exploration of the geological strata of our fossiliferous words.

xxv

Whether or not the words acquire the luster they once had, the strategies of theatre over the next fifteen years will be conceived after the spacious model of *language*. Whatever the linchpin with the body, the body cannot think of the future, as only language does—which has the amplitude we long for, and the indeterminacy, in its precisions. If there is also an accrual of the fabulous around the nominalism, a mythicizing of the model, that may be because whatever there was in the beginning, with or without the Word, there is still the theoretical suspicion that there would be no theatre without it, no future, and no theory. The etymological linchpin between theatre and theory is in the place and act of watching; that is, *speculation*, even before the words were sounded, as with the basilisk in the garden reading the situation, that smooth talker, *hypocrite lecteur*—the first actor?

xxvi

If the quickest eye is in the mind, and words as swift as thought, the quick objects of the mind are not, in the gross actual world, as moveable as thought. So with the more superconducting cybernetic illusions. Post-industrialization, with its pure brain theory realized in silicon chips, will probably have to wait on re-industrialization (hopefully not as dull as the Democrats, with their long commitment to the unions, make it sound), blue-collar workers with old-fashioned muscle-power. And nothing is better suited to reflect that than the theatre, with its long tradition of manual labor and new vocabulary of ideographic sweat.

xxvii

The sculptor Richard Serra has given us, however, a suggestive image of postmodern reconversion of heavy industry—long past the early modern romance of the machine or the facile new deconstructing parodies—in his film of a railroad turnbridge, where the graceful architectural swivel of the track is no mere exercise in perception like, for instance, his own earlier film *Frame* (1969). (The development is taken farther in the documentary about the forging of his 70-ton cube in a German steel mill, which includes interviews with the workers whose relationship to the oppressiveness of their work is not changed by the presence of sculpture, though they are quite able to perceive that it's "a work of art to bend a shaft, to forge it nicely.") Whatever the film does for the dialogue of art history out of which so much art, and perfor-

mance, is being made, it also reminds us, like Serra's precariously lean-
ing lead plates, of what in the predictable future we are most likely to
be living with, and without the relief of an easy condescension to
replace the lapsed nostalgia.

xxviii

The swivel has an affinity with the camera trackings of Michael
Snow, but with more implicit social "content," in the simple arc of the
pivoting turnbridge from a projection of motion back to *use*
and—despite the first and last images of unencumbered
space—without the ruined imperialism of a site-specific distance
(Smithson, Heizer) that only those who can afford it can ever really
see, except on film or in gallery documentation. This uselessness, converted by artists to, say, a coverup for strip mining, is the theme of a recent disconsolate essay by Robert Morris on land reclamation: "What,
one wonders, could be done for the Kennecott Bingham site, the
ultimate site-specific work of such raging, ambitious energy, so
redolent with formal power and social threat, that no existing earth
work should even be compared to it?" His own virtuoso energy is no
match, nor does he have an answer, except to remind us that art has
always been a destructive force, without morality, serving pharoahs
and mammon as well as saints. "If the only rule is that art must use
what uses it, then one would not be put off by the generally high level
of idiocy, politics, and propaganda attached to public
monuments—especially if one is in the business of erecting them."

xxix

It's been a while since theatre has been in such a business. At least in
this country, and not in the grandiose ascetic spirit of Artaud's "No
More Masterpieces." If Artaud wasn't thinking of monuments, he was
certainly thinking of ruins. It was never a question of scale. One of our
theatre's problems, that of scale, is that nobody is going to underwrite
anything like those lead plates of Serra, no less a 70-ton steel cube. It
wasn't quite the same when in the Cultural Explosion of the fifties, the
fringe benefits of a permanent war economy put up a number of
buildings for Regional Theatres whose stability is still either too uncertain or too incurably mediocre to even think of such a problem. When
we think of scale in American theatre today, we might remember that
Lee Breuer has taken over a football field or that Robert Wilson has
received financing for the magnitude of his projects, once at Persepolis,
once at the Met; but if his gift is idiosyncratic, it is also remarkably en-
trepreneurial, and the subsidy is now mostly from Germany, where

magnitude has been the mode and the problem is scaling down—the most experimental directors worrying along revived Marcusean lines about preëmptive tolerance in the large state theatres which support their work. Here—with funds dwindling and the touring circuit narrowing with the budgets—some of our more experimental directors are probably quite ready, like Morris with Kennecott Bingham, to go into business; if not with Broadway, then with the Regional Theatres, covering up the vacancies, if they can ever really afford it. I don't think much of this will really be happening, not on anything like the German scale, in the next fifteen years. Earthworks, like Performance Art, which came out of the desire to outflank the gallery system, were reappropriated by that system, whose possibilities of lucrative patronage are not yet available even for the best practitioners in the experimental theatre. Nor can the disappearing continuity of companies be mapped and photographed, like Christo's running fence, for sale, when it is no longer there.

xxx

But leaving the almost unreclaimable landscape to the longer dimensions of time—when it may be, according to some future-thinkers, impossible to distinguish between technological and biological forms—let us return to the large-scale felicities of Serra's film. For us in the theatre, it is interesting because it allows itself what Serra does not allow in his sculpture, whose massive minimalism still refuses representation (which doesn't mean it can be successfully refused). While the sculpture is allied to theatre by its physicality in space, the film is closer to theatre through the play of analogy, its trafficking with appearance, the duplicitous substance of theatre, still, however, keeping it at a distance because it is focussed on the outside world, the bridge, a social artifact whose designation as such is never formally obscured in the site-specificity of its perceptual transformations. As a reflection on technology, it shares the circular momentum, from the turn of the bridge to outer space, of Wilson's *Einstein on the Beach*, but is without the autistic surrealist patina. Nor does it have, in the social impulse that led (somewhat accidentally) to *Steelmill*, anything like the cultish politicism of Joseph Beuys, with its invented aura of a personal myth of origins. It is nominalist, with scale, not asocial, neither anachronizing nor derogating its materials—and I should like to see more of it in the theatre.

xxxi

With the caveats about a technology registered in the computer but waiting its turn, we should also remember that there is a sense in which there is no such thing as *innovation* in the theatre (after the second actor, and the third) except at the level of *external* technology, starting with the mask and costume, musical instruments (as both sound and scenic utensils), and then some other semblance of scenery, perioktoi or eccyclema, properties, the startling obtrusion of a curtain (possibly the major innovation in theatre history), and then the mechanisms for changing the stage or moving the platforms or superimposing light or, now, electronically turning the tables or mixing the media. But it's apparent that none of these things are *in themselves* of the essence or, if so, as historical moments which may be—as by withdrawing the curtain and letting it drop again, or cutting it in half—recapitulated. And whenever we find ourselves redefining the theatre or projecting its future, if the mechanisms get in the way we will get rid of the mechanisms, in favor of the naked stage or the poor theatre with the naked actor, which are now—like shifting the theatre back to the landscape—also historical moments.

xxxii

Recapitulating: To the degree that we began to suspect that the drama, like the dematerialized technology, was a mechanism of power, a duplicitous structure of appearances, we tried to get rid of the drama, about whose true nature we have been arguing since Aristotle—though the argument about the theatre went back to the immaterial presences in Plato's cave.

xxxiii

Actually, the theatre can only sustain itself so long in either direction, with too much drama (melodrama) or without it (plot exposed, banished, or scattered), *as spectacle*, whether with mechanical technology or the naked actor, depending on the speculation in the spectacle, and the quality of its voyeurism, the power of its specular obsessions—as if Aristotle, who seems far afield from the indeterminacy in the eye of the beholder and the contemporary breakdown of conceptual categories, had anticipated it all, including film, when he wrote in *De Anima* that "the activity of the sensible object and that of the percipient sense is one and the same activity."

xxxiv

To the degree that the theatre's future is bound up with developments in technology, it will not have evacuated itself of the idea of progress, which has been its subject matter through the history of the avant-garde. The belief in radical change on a progressive axis is always contradicted, however, by the equally radical regressions of the avant-garde, essentially reactionary, but doubly so in the theatre, because of the inherently skeptical nature of the form. Why skeptical? What else can it be, fastened as it is to a dying animal, the mystery of whose self-consciously absurd persistence never leaves the stage, even if the stage is scattered like, today, the belief in a continuous self, and the animal is no longer there. If the mystery is not there, whatever else it may be, it will not be theatre. Yet we live in a period of demystifications, severely distrustful of theatre—source of the self's illusions and the illusory self—and given to *theatricality* as a means of disarticulating the mystery (the "that within that passeth show"), whose origins are dubious, ghostly, and whose end is never in sight, though you can feel it coming, thereby obscuring the moment, by arousing false desire.

xxxv

Which is always desiring desire: the memory of (an illusory?) gratification which can never be appeased, the future always denying the instant. In recent years, we have had performance events which have tried to preserve the integrity of the instant by minimizing or cooling down desire, which is presumably tricked into being by ideology, which is what the mystery is really about. The egocentric actor doing his part didn't always know it, and thus became its corrupted and corrupting agent. (I suppose that's why they were cautious about introducing more than one actor, one ego was enough.) There were always those who felt something like that: Craig, who wanted his puppets, and Duse, who wanted to kill all the actors and start over. Brecht—wanting only to restrain them, not intending to minimize the human presence—nevertheless gave us, in our time, the cue for more distrust, warning us about the emotion which implied a future which is *overdetermined,* and therefore in its fated cadence unsusceptible to change.

xxxvi

In trying to *construct* a future with no ontological mystification, we have sometimes tried to forget that in some timewarped corner of remembrance there may still be something interminably waiting (*in* the technology but *not* the technology) to trammel up the consequence. The kind of theatre we may do in the future depends upon just how illusory we think that is. Or how afraid of it we are, assenting or denying, so that we develop our own mechanisms in self-defense, which also resemble theatre structures (Acconci, Anderson). For want of certain knowledge about the remembrance, the emphasis has been in the theatre and other performance events upon the clarifying task or structure, with more or less psychic content, sometimes expressionist and autobiographical, more or less desperate (Gray, Montano), in more or less "real-time"—but equivocating between *presentness* (as in the presentness of the past) and, whether cooled down or heated up, a desire for *presence* with no illusions. And we want it right *now*, undisguised, though it always seems to be putting us off.

xxxvi

(And the more we think about it, the more dreadful it is, and maybe it's just as well:)

xxxviii

For the presence we seem unable to engender—what drove Artaud mad—seems to exist somewhere between the libido and death, the imagining of which arrests us, though we can't seem to do anything with it except, in fact, to *theatricalize* it. And that's not a *living* death but only living theatre, and not (though we momentarily thought it was) the presence we want. The unrepresentability of our own death keeps us—for all the continuing sentiment about carnivals, festivals, participatory environments and the millenarian promise of full participation, with no separation between the dancer and the dance—always in the position of spectators. It is maddening, but the theatre will never run out of a future so long as it's driven by that.

xxxix

Model for a New Theatre, from the unicorn tapestries, in *The Notebooks of Malte Laurids Brigge:* "But here is yet another festival; no one is invited to it. Expectation plays no part in it. Everything is here. Everything for ever. The lion looks around almost threateningly: no one may come. We have never yet seen her weary; is she weary? Or has she only seated herself because she is holding something heavy? A monstrance, one might think. But she curves her other arm toward the unicorn, and the creature bridles, flattered, and rears and leans upon her lap. It is a mirror, the thing she holds. See: she is showing the mirror its image—.

"Abelone, I am imagining that you are here. Do you understand, Abelone? I think you must understand."

xl

.The dread we set aside in the parenthesis of being arises from the possibility that we will be driven into a future in which we are no longer spectators, quite the opposite of the ultimate participatory desire. In Freud, as Lacoue-Labarthe has pointed out, theatricality as matrix occurs not in the analytical sense (and hence beyond the beginnings of the cathartic method) but "in the metapsychology itself: in the irreducible dualism of the drives." It is the analysis that reveals, in the perceptual space of Plato's scenography, the philosophic desire for mastery (the Royal Road), "the 'basilic' desire at work in the philosophical *deflection* of tragedy."

xli

In the popular Nietzscheanism of the last generation, we thought to release the Dionysian, and then, when that exhausted itself in the turbulence of the late sixties, to once again reconcile Dionysus and Apollo. But what is not quite Nietzschean, even as the polymorphous perversity wore off, is the assumption that Apollo needs to be invoked as the upholder of representation against the bararians who would shatter the icons, obliterate metaphor, smash analogy, rape the Symbolic and, in the terrorism of total theatre, bring an end to theatre. But Nietzsche, who studied Dionysus to his own living end, did to that enigmatic god what Marx did to Hegel and what, in Euripides' play, the god did to Pentheus, turned him upside down. For he realized, as did Euripides in *The Bacchae* (but not in some of the versions we have seen), that "it is within the Dionysian itself," as Lacoue-Labarthe puts it, "that the *interdiction* of presence takes place, or, to put it in another language (one that Freud uses in an enigmatic text ['On Transience'] to justify the desire of art), death incessantly undermines and deports 'presence' irrevocably, dooming us to repetition."

xlii

Probably, we should have been discouraged. But what we heard a generation ago in the necrophilic desire of *Endgame* was an apocalyptic summons to the postmodern (call it what you will, Beckett called it the Unnameable), the longing prospect of a future which is ceaselessly deferred and—as they said for similar chastening reasons in Action Painting, though wanting to leave a mark—*allover*, through the secretion or expulsion of pain into a more spacious universe which, in Beckett, was contracted to a needle's eye.

xliii

"Who, if I cried," said Rilke in the first elegy, "would hear me among the angelic/orders?" If we remember correctly (and the Classical Anthropologists, through all rationalistic error, touched some nerve-end of origins) the theatre was born of such a cry taking its chances. Over the last fifteen years, along with the toning down of desire in some of our art, there was a compulsion of *innateness*, evangelized by Artaud and methodized by Grotowski, to experiment with the birthright and raise the cry again. If there is one tendency of the postmodern to thwart disguise by keeping it all on the surface, there is another wanting to scourge it by having it all out, confessionally, palpably, to the point of exhaustion, ripping through the vocal chords to the source of Utterance, if only in theory now, the gristled and muzzling *"writing aloud"* (Barthes) of the carnal actor of Artaud, the stereophony of an avenging angel, bereft, outscreaming the paradisal wind.

xliv

The trouble with confession, beyond the candor, is that there may not be as much as you think, not all that much to say, depending on the resources of experience and will that—though we want desperately to believe the opposite—not everybody has. So there you are again wanting to make it up or, as with the interpretation of dreams, not sure whether it's confessing *or* making it up, and once you admit that, then there's more than you can possibly say—and that, too, is finding its way into the theatre. There can't, however, be an answer to the question of *identity*—the motive of innateness, the solipsist's desire—until we take up again (not in the standard dramatic forms, nor the institutional theatres, but within this matrix of thought) the possible proposition that someone is there who insists upon being answered, and that the voice which wants to be answered doesn't always come from within.

xlv

That was not the case with the primal scream. It was quickly exhausted. So were the hieratic incantations, which all sounded so much alike, like the answers which come before the question. The cry has since diminished in its intensity, subsiding from Persepolis into the murmurs of history, paratheatrical solemnities in the forest, the network of underground or solo performances, and the infatuations of theatricality in everday life which seem to make theatre redundant, though it may not be getting through the noise. And the angels may be tired of listening and the orders no longer there, and the metatheatrical tendency of the postmodern is to ignore it (with inflections of pain, sometimes exorbitant, or with "minimalist reduction"—which doesn't mean it doesn't hurt—in Body Art), playing with the arbitrariness of the signifiers in the insufferable debris.

xlvi

Blown about the wreckage, we return to the *bricolage*. In the systems of estrangement, we strain to read the signs. In the prophetic soul of the wide world dreaming on things to come, it is important to remember that whatever experiment is currently going on in the theatre is still playing out the consequences of an intimidating history—all the more so because of an increasing *theoretical* emphasis in the arts and other disciplines on radical discontinuity, taking epistemologically for granted about "the universe of discourse" what the scientists are cosmologically debating about the universe of quasars and charmed quarks. It is a debate which hasn't come to any conclusion since Einstein remarked about Heisenberg's principle of indeterminacy that God doesn't play dice with the cosmos. For want of any conclusiveness in the cosmos, the ethos of discontinuity, which is a refusal of the inseminating Word, is a perhaps necessary counter-fiction to the falsifying cadence of an illusory coherence. But it is something other than what Wallace Stevens meant by the Necessary Angel—an imagination pressing back against the pressure of the real, mastery of words in a world made (so far as we know) out of words, which have returned to the theatre, but with nothing like the stature they had, and surrounded by critical subversions of the Authorizing Text. If we listen to the theory, the Text is the rubble of the wreckage, a catastrophe in itself.

xlvii

"I can't be punished anymore." Would it were so. What Clov insists upon, equivocally, pausing over the heap, may refer to the words themselves, maybe yes maybe no, in the prison-house of language (Nietzsche), where the same oedipal story is forever being told. The desire to unburden the theatre of that story—with its supporting apparatus of domination and power, hierarchy, the mortifying Name of the Father, and what one feminist calls "the megalo-sexist dreams" with "the same old shit, pus, blood, sperm (oh! come on!)," and the incest taboo—is a consummation (perhaps) devoutly to be wished, *if* it is wished, and if it *is* (conceding, through so much insistence, a point which is still illegible on the mystic writing pad), whether or not it would really be liveable were it consummated.

xlviii

The necessity of the phallocentric shadow remains an open question (mouthing or yawning like the grave) which is still determining the future of the theatre, through the depredations upon the old drama and the legitimacy of the Plot, the deconstructions of the narrative with its family romance, and the revisionist history of a woman's world, where there's still no doubt about the pain. "This is Electra speaking," says the voice of Ophelia, in a wheelchair—in Heiner Müller's *The Hamletmachine*, her body being wrapped in gauze as "fish, debris, dead bodies and limbs drift by." After the Ice Age, a sperm-ejected world, beyond Brecht, with his alienating cool. "I choke between my thighs the world I gave birth to. I bury it in my womb. Down with the happiness of submission. Long live hate and comtempt, rebellion and death. When she walks through your bedrooms carrying butcher knives you'll know the truth." The terrible irony would be, not even then.

xlix

Nor is it the first vision we've had of the death of theatre in the terminal revolution, or the birth of theatre in the ecstasy of carnage. And of course there's a difference between saying it and doing it, and in any case *"Ophelia remains on stage, motionless in her white wrappings,"* and Müller is male and East German and fighting personal battles through the maimed figure of the woman, *using* her again for his own political purposes, as she was used in the old Plot. The actor-who-plays-Hamlet destroys the portraits of Marx, Lenin, and Mao with the poleax of the Father, after being instructed with all the Author's self-contempt to tear up the photograph of the Author, who is trying to find *his* way honorably into the future behind the hideous Wall, by surrendering his identity, and his text, to a process on the other side of history; which is to say, in the unconscious, the staging-place of the permanent revolution, which respects neither time, identity, nor death. As long as we're on that other stage, however, on the other side of the Wall . . .

l

. . . what happened to Electra? For the moment she is exorcising the ancient fury more tellingly on film, which is, at least in this century, the entrancing locus of her dispossession (as of feminist theory), the fantasy-making apparatus itself, the inoculated stock (exchange) of absence, where the unwrapped image of the woman's body has been, for a handsome profit, so deceptively alluring and so mortally abused.

li

It was surely the blindness of Constructivism to the impending deconstructions that caused Meyerhold (teacher of Eisenstein), later erased from the encyclopedia, to speak of "that detestable rectangle, the screen." For there, without the testing presence of the corporeal actor, in a dematerializing fiction of projected light (as if going through Marx's *Grundrisse* to the dream's navel, where Freud is being remembered, and reinterpreted, through the radicalized hysteria of his patient Dora), the whole libidinal economy could be torn apart, organs spilling through the delirium of the slit eye until, cutting to the brain, there is only the illumined blank screen itself with its empty images, another festival, pure naked intensities circling unbetrayed, not the gross and agglutinative body of surplus value, but the very apotheosis of *lack*, untouchable by the codes of social production, all germens spilling at once, "*No mouth. No tongue. No teeth. No larynx. No esophagus. No belly. No anus.*"—Artaud's wishfulfilling antioedipal nightmare come true. (See the dreams of Dr. Schreber, or Deleuze and Guattari.) The theatre can't achieve anything like this so long as the actor, at the sacrificial end of all longing, with the last unpurged seizure of arrested id, insists through the vertiginous litanies of the self's disappearance, the body ready, thawed, and resolved into a dew, on the residual vanity of a Real Presence.

lii

The trouble with the theatre is that, if the actor is *there* (and we are seeing theatre without actors), too much artfulness is required—as concealment or unconcealment—to mediate the problem with Electra, who is speaking for the victims of illusion, who are crying out for no more theatre. The theatre has taken the cry to heart, but what can it do but theatre? Whether theatre is a phantom of ideology (Marx) or ideology a phantom of theatre (Bacon), the theatre is in an ideological double bind—which may be what it is to *be* theatre, and I suspect we'll see more of that. I mean more thinking about it in the theatre over the next fifteen years. Even when the theatre is being candid about its theatricality, it always seems fake. That's the problem, we saw it in Brecht, the actor is always pretending, even when he's pretending he's not. The purer appearances of film seem realer, because the actor isn't there, only his image, whereas in the theatre the actor is there *with* his image, like the "unperfect actor on the stage" in the other sonnet, "Who with his fear is *put besides* his part. . . ." The emphasis is mine, and it is a very strange ontological problem. Even Shakespeare didn't understand it, though he knew enough to make it the center of his theatre, which is why he remains even now, despite Brecht's critique and subsequent deconstructions, close to our best intuitions of what the theatre *is*.

liii

If the actor isn't there in the theatre, we seem to be evading the problem and the theatre seems a little anemic. The more arduous theatre of the future—I mean a theatre equal to our love of the truth we can no longer believe in or adequately embody in any gender that we yet know, that is, *the truth of the actor*—will come, I think, out of the other end of this theoretical dilemma. I wish I could be confident that it will only take fifty years. Nietzsche thought, starting about twice fifty years ago, that "this is the great spectacle in a hundred acts reserved for the next two centuries in Europe—the most terrible, the most questionable, and perhaps also the most helpful of all spectacles." We used to do things faster in America, so perhaps we're nearing a solution, though I doubt it (or fear it), but here's how he puts the theatrical issue, not sure that he has an audience: "what meaning would *our* whole being possess if it were not this, that in us the will to truth becomes conscious of itself as a *problem?*"

liv

After more than half a century of intensely self-conscious theatre, theatre about theatre, its discourse and modes of production, the whole illusory apparatus of deception, it would seem we've played through all the phallocratic horns of the dilemma. But there is still the double bind (propounded by Pirandello and doubled over by Genet), and my impression is that we have only played around with it in recent years, as conundrum, parody, concept, more or less polysemous, in successive etiolations of the play-within-the-play, forgetting that the play is not only *within*, innate, but within *the play*—with the inevitable trivialization, in the autonomy of play, of the *idea* of play itself.

lv

As a result, the actor—at precisely the time he has been liberated from the realistic constraints that are more endemic to the cinema, and from servitude to the Director, the Playwright, and the authoritarian Text—finds himself, with a more limber body and a new ideographic expressiveness, not really knowing what there is to say, as in the vapidity of the recent *Re-Arrangements*, where charter members of The Open Theater seemed to be rehearsing pallid and spastic versions of themselves up to their old games, with a sort of bittersweet schmalziness they would have once derided in The Actor's Studio, as if in disavowing the self-indulgent Method the method of physical actions were playing the Superobjective backwards. Even with more time on stage, in self-determining structures, there is now a peculiar sensation that our actors have a somewhat diminished function, less to do than it first seemed when they were released from the old script—not unlike what instrumental musicians experienced (actors never had their training) with the emergence of atonal music, a sense of virtuosity wasted (when they did get some training) in an excess of what was required.

lvi

There are nowadays new performers, like Stuart Sherman and John Zorn, who have created personal scores independent of the old notion of a text. And this has been a period of Performance Art—in theatre and the galleries and other sites—where along with the emphasis on highly-trained *performers* (the word has been preferred to *actor*) we have also cultivated the amateur, and developed events for participants without professional skills. Over the next fifteen years we will continue to see performance pieces with non-actors, or without actors, in a staging of (unpejoratively intended) bloodless objects seeking a subject, as the characters once sought the Author. He was actually still very much there at the time, on the periphery, before he was drummed out of the theatre by the dissidence of the sixties, which thought it was distributing the power, and dismembered ever since by the sparagmos of theory, which is subliminally running the show, or holding it in escrow until "the closure of representation" (Derrida on Artaud).

lvii

Out of earlier dispersions of the Text—which lost the characters who were searching for the Author—came other diversionary strategies that we will continue to see in a sometimes elegant "landscape play" of disjunctions, whose tutelary deities are Cage, Duchamp and Gertrude

Stein, who gave us the term. Aside from the actor/performer making allegories of objects or minimalist musical scores or hiding under puppets, we have had events in which the actors themselves are philosophical "partial objects" or the structural equivalents of objects, with the same status as the legendary orange attached by string to a chair. It is a phenomenological reduction of a formally ingenious kind in, say, the work of Richard Foreman. Through systems of repetition—for instance, the cinematic recurrencies of the non-character Rhoda—previously untrained performers have acquired appropriate skills. In Foreman's autocratic surveillance, if there's liberation from the old Text, there is—for the one who is playing Rhoda—servitude to the new, surrendering the actor's autonomy to the *event*. From "one small seed could burgeon an enormous tree"—but for one of the oldest characters lurking in the background, this particular reduction is not the one. For it is another kind of allegory in which, for objects and actors alike, destiny is deliberately ruined. While it might not drive her to rage, Electra can only mourn.

lviii

"And that is that," says her mother, after the deadly glory of "the birthtime of the buds," the tree axed in the tub, in another landscape of disjunctions, utterly reduced. What the theatre is, and may be, is summed up in the distance between Clytemnestra's royal carpet, through which is mantically woven the indelible winds of Aulis, and Cage's ephemeral curtain, which unfurls a musicating theatre in a momentary breeze. The carpet and the curtain are, however, furnishings of the same history, totalizing concepts of theatre. As far apart as they appear to be—through centuries of innumerable transformations and now unnameable forms—there doesn't seem to be much room for another major alternative. Not in the near future, nor yet imagined by a woman; if we *are* still speaking of theatre and not the Unnameable itself.

lix

The halfway measures were most acutely suggested by the half-curtain of Brecht borrowed from the theatre of the Far East, which keeps you at a distance by presumably letting you in on the secret; or like the Kathakali (from which we've recently borrowed acting techniques), headdress above and feet below, and mystery in the middle regions where, with genesis still at the genitals, the theatre comes out of trance. There is still talk about trance, but like the instant mantras of the Counter-Culture, it has temporarily played itself out in the shamans and hungans of the New Theatre. As for the Kathakali, it has had a long-nurtured ascetic discipline and a traditional heritage of signs to sustain its mesmeric intensities, feet stamping the floor, while the eyes play moonlike over the landscape. It is no longer propitious. In a post-industrial world, it will be adulterated by over-exposure. As western images travel from New Delhi to Kerala, there will be inevitable changes in the desire that shapes and sustains images.

lx

And so, all over the world, whatever the forms of desire, the figure in the carpet is worn. As the current story goes, it has faded like origins into the sometimes barely perceptible, undiachronic but not unsystematic inflexions of indeterminacy in everyday life, where the self has been dissociating itself as theatre. Or, with various degrees of anxiety and mastery, resisting the pressures of the real, into the suspensions, conspiracies or final solutions of Silence. But while there has been a lot of high-powered propaganda about the disappearance of the ego-centered self, along with the humanistic image of man, the figure in the carpet is obdurate if not decipherable, and at least surreptitiously there. The issues of authorship and the authority of the Text are caught up in the threads like Agamemnon in the polymorphous net. Almost all controversy over what the theatre should be has to do—from the cavity of Plato's iridescent thought to any conceivable future without mimesis—with the propriety of its lingering presence. Of the most consequential theatre that will be, at conscious and subliminal levels, the unavoidable subject—as if corresponding to the reëmergence of the Middle East, where the carpet was first woven and the theatre seems to have been born.

lxi

Meanwhile, we permutate the hybrids. In an age of systematic hybridization, that's mostly what we'll continue to do through the next generation and into the next century, whether in the spectacular, or somnambulant, dimensions of opera, or the slapstick disjunctures of movie-like collage, doubly mixing the media, or in underground or solo performances by troupes of communitarian anarchists or actors like standup comedians with nothing but themselves on stage or with talismanic personal objects, hermetically arrayed, in lofts living rooms factories sidewalks (the quality of the politics in the streets depending on the stage of industrialization of the political setting), in feminist collectives, or with suggestions of terrorism, or summoning up defunct myths in abandoned gas stations, with masks and puppets, like a palimpsest of all these, oneirically at the edge of the sea.

lxii

The subject of the theatre, as I have written elsewhere, is not only the illusion of a future but the future of illusion, which is still blowing through history in that paradisal gaze. Outside the normal precincts of theatre, in the minimalist proclivities of Performance Art, the objective was to put the question of illusion up front, settling it once and for all, on the *surface*—which, even without actors, turned out to be a very porous mass. With actors, or in Body Art, it bleeds into itself as in Kafka's Penal Colony, skin scraped by metaphysics—or retreats into the unconscious, where all the wreckage has settled, a Moebius topography of ruinations which refuses to be leveled out. As for the ecstatic extremities of Artaud's vision—the actor like an angel signalling through the flames—they have largely tapered off in practice, while being, as I've suggested, hypostatized in theory. The sonorous body of his own forked thought inscribed upon our brains, however, the prospect of a theatre as a ruthless physiology of signs matching Marx's ruthless critique of everything existing, with the illusion of its being nakedly attainable, like the memory of a second Creation. The legacy of the alchemical vision, with its unremitting desire to pulverize all the mediating signs, still seems to be impelling Grotowski but, after his visit to America, as if by way of Esalen into a kind of Gothic Gestalt. His paratheatrical activity since *Holiday* is sure to be emulated in this country in the ever-recurring novelty of a congenital primitivism which would dematerialize the last remaining distances between art and life.

lxiii

Those distances remain, however, as thick as time, narrowed as they may be by Occam's razor—like the cuticles of the fingernails holding on for dear life, refusing to relinquish it to total theatre. At the same time, the desire for still another ideogram, the last word, annulling the distance, will persist—and sometimes with a poignancy coming through its most comic manifestations, as in Calvino's cosmic fantasies: "I wanted immediately to make a new sign in space that would make Kgwgk die of envy"—where, in the unnameable other worlds, we have the intensity of the pure desire and its old earthly human contradiction.

lxiv

What we will see, I think, in the next half century, is an intricate distancing of that desire, a playing out of the refusal in the contradiction and the contradiction of the refusal, arrested at each end by our new awareness of the possible forms of play, which is never gratuitous: mimetic and methetic, frank artifice and utter naturalism, inner and outer, announced play and disguised pretense, surface and depth, alienation and empathy, the secret *and* its exposure, not merely as oscillations but as *infiltrations*. What we are coming to realize—with resistances that are human and ideological, and no doubt in-eliminable—is that *all of these are appearances of the other*, erasures allusions perturbations corrections misprisions overlays reversals and provisional end stops. All of them will lead, when pressed to the utmost logic of the most illusory desire, around the not-quite synchronous edges of the metamorphic circle—the actor looking at himself or being looked at, looking at herself looking, in a new consciousness, labile and feminine but not unpatriarchal, of the available spectrum of acting (if not action), playing off the incremental concepts of person self role subject character persona mask, with no impediment between the im-provisational and the analytical, between doing it and thinking it. We have learned after years of understated method that to act less is sometimes to act more, more or less, depending on where you are in history, the future in the seed.

lxv

The acting will appear self-reflective or presentational, decentered or umbilical, at a hallucinatory distance or clinically close up, as a subjective drama of presence, or an objectifying narrative in the second or third person which is absorbed before you know it in the hallucinatory stream. Or there will be purported event irrespective of person, through concrete tasks or hypothetical objectives, with the pro-missory insistence that there are no strings attached. But there will be the recension of a lot of writing between the lines that will, probably, be spoken more and more, in the exposures of ideology, *as images*, de-nying the exposure, each playing off the other in a calculus of percep-tions, shadows doubles projections intimations of prospective behavior, playing with identity or identifying the prospect of play, since the one thing that can no longer be the same is the pretense that there is only the one way—though if we'd followed the angel of history through the backward movement of time, studying the theatre's changes, we would have known it was only a pretense and that, in order to liberate the theatre in the future, we may have to arbitrarily pretend again.

lxvi

Today we are pretending, some of us, that we can do away with illusion, and thus with the substance of theatre, even while we are pretending that performance is the means. It is a remarkable proposition in its most strenuous theoretical form. I think it is the most interesting proposition about the theatre. There is, however, a self-evident logic which the assault on representation would undermine, that says the theatre's future is in *remaining theatre*, and making the most of that illusion. But to know what it is to want the remainder you have to approach the illusory edge where it hardly seems to matter, the most duplicitous moment of all. When the theatre looks to the future, it always comes back to that. There may be more desirable states of being than that obscured by the duplicity, but in imitating nature—as the theatre irreparably does—the theatre is the illusion of what appears to be left of life.